ROMANS
A DEVOTIONAL COMMENTARY

ROMANS

A DEVOTIONAL COMMENTARY

BO GIERTZ

TRANSLATED BY
BROR ERICKSON

EXCERPTED FROM
THE NEW TESTAMENT DEVOTIONAL
COMMENTARIES SERIES.

Romans: A Devotional Commentary

© 2018 Bror Erickson for the English translation

All rights reserved. No part of this publication may be reproduced, distributed, or transmitted in any form or by any means, including photocopying, recording, or other electronic or mechanical methods, without the prior written permission of the publisher, except in the case of brief quotations embodied in critical reviews and certain other noncommercial uses permitted by copyright law. For permission requests, write to the publisher at the address below.

Published by:
NRP Books
PO Box 54032
Irvine, CA 92619–4032

Cover design by Brenton Clarke Little

Printed in the United States of America

Publisher's Cataloging-In-Publication Data
(Prepared by The Donohue Group, Inc.)

Names: Giertz, Bo, 1905–1998. | Erickson, Bror, translator.
Title: Romans : a devotional commentary / Bo Giertz ; translated by Bror Erickson.
Other Titles: Förklaringar till Nya testamentet. Andra Delen, Johannesevangeliet, Apostlagärningarna, Romarbrevet, Korinterbreven. Selections. English
Description: Irvine, CA : 1517 Publishing, [2018] | "Excerpted from the New Testament devotional commentaries series." | Translation of commentary extracted from Förklaringar till Nya testamentet. Andra Delen, Johannesevangeliet, Apostlagärningarna, Romarbrevet, Korinterbreven. | Includes bibliographical references and index.
Identifiers: ISBN 9781945978678 (hardcover) | ISBN 9781945978685 (softcover) | ISBN 9781945978692 (ebook)
Subjects: LCSH: Bible. Romans—Commentaries. | Bible. Romans—Devotional literature.
Classification: LCC BS2665.3 .G5413 2018 (print) | LCC BS2665.3 (ebook) | DDC 227/.107—dc23

NRP Books, an imprint of 1517 the Legacy Project, is committed to packaging and promoting the finest content for fueling a new Lutheran Reformation. We promote the defense of the Christian faith, confessional Lutheran theology, vocation and civil courage.

Contents

Introduction 1

Romans 1 9

Romans 2 17

Romans 3 21

Romans 4 27

Romans 5 31

Romans 6 35

Romans 7 41

Romans 8 47

Romans 9 53

Romans 10 59

Romans 11 63

Romans 12 69

Romans 13 75

Romans 14 79

Romans 15 83

Romans 16 87

Introduction

The Letters of Paul

In our Bibles, the thirteen letters of Paul follow right after Acts. This has been the case since antiquity. It is a peculiarity if one finds a manuscript in which they are not in the same place as they are today. We have no traces of manuscripts that contain only Paul's letters or just a few of them.[1] It is apparent that they had been gathered together at an early stage and that even then the thirteen letters took the order in which they are still read today. First come "congregational letters" and then follow the letters to individuals, and each group is arranged according to length so that the longest comes first. This is the reason Romans comes first in the series.

We also have reason to believe that this was the only collection of Paul's letters in antiquity. It is in this form that they were known and read ever since congregations began to desire them. We know that it was common to collect letters in this way, as happened with the letters that the martyr Bishop Ignatius of Antioch wrote when he was taken to Rome as a prisoner around 110 AD. Even this very collection reached Asia Minor, appearing in the same districts where we have reason to believe that this collection of Paul's letters was already in existence.

When a congregation received a letter from Paul, it would obviously be read during the divine service. If it was a long letter like

---

[1] Paul's letters have most often been found grouped together with Acts and the general letters. See http://trobisch.com/david/wb/media/material/PaulsLetterCollection%20chapter%201.pdf, 11.

Romans, it could take many Sundays. At times, we hear Paul instruct the readers that his letters should also be read in the neighboring congregation and that one should see to it that the letter he sent there is shared (Col 4:16). This in itself could have been reason enough to copy the letter. Otherwise, especially during the early years, those who received the letters may have been less scrupulous about taking care of them.

The letters to the Corinthians mention at least two letters that have been lost. But Paul was still alive at that time; the recipients still expected that he would visit and they would be able to listen to him personally. The situation was different after his death. The letters one might have from Paul were irreplaceable. They were read in the divine service. They were copied and in demand in the congregations. Finally, they were collected in the form we now have them.

We don't exactly know when it happened. But because they were diligently cited in the Christian writings during the first half of the second century, one figures that the collection must have come together sometime around the year 100 or maybe even earlier.

Real Letters

Paul's letters are real letters. They were sent to particular addressees via willing couriers or some of the apostle's coworkers, some of whom we know by name. Paul sent the letters to Ephesus and Colossae with Tychicus, the deaconess Phoebe probably carried Romans, and Titus carried Second Corinthians.

Normally, one wrote on papyrus. A short letter—the length of John's second or third letter—might fit on a single page of papyrus. But the little letter of Philemon, the shortest we have from Paul's hand, must have demanded two. The pages would be pasted together edge to edge. In the end, "the letter" could be a couple meters long. One only wrote on one side, letting the text follow column upon column from left to right. When the letter was finished, it was rolled up and sealed, and the address was written on the outside.

As a rule, Paul seems to have dictated his letters to a scribe. We know that the scribe who wrote Romans for him was named Tertius because he also sent a greeting. When Paul's dictation was finished, he would usually take the pen himself and write a greeting with his own hand.

Thus Paul's letters are not small tracts or theses that were written with the idea that they should be given wider circulation. Books in the form of letters were actually well-known and popular literature in antiquity. In the New Testament, this style is represented by the Catholic Letters. But when Paul writes, he has particular recipients in mind. He is speaking to them. He is taking up their problems and questions. He does not need to mention them because they are already known to the readers. For this reason, it can often be difficult for us to truly understand what he is speaking about.

Historical Documents

Paul's letters are an invaluable source of knowledge concerning the first decades of Christianity. They were written within the second or third decade after Christ's death, between the years 50 and 65. They allow us to encounter the apostle's conflicts, worries, and joys just as they were experienced by him when the letters were written. In a manner of speaking, a letter is like a photograph. It can give us a momentary picture of one man and his environment, captured in a given situation, often with details that would otherwise never have come to our knowledge. At the same time, we are able to see the past in a manner that is seldom the case with a historical retrospective. We get authentic firsthand information without intermediaries screening and ordering things.

One does not always think about what an outstanding historical source we have here when it comes to basic facts about Jesus. To begin with, we can remove all the unrealistic claims that Jesus has never lived or that we cannot know anything about Him for sure. Here we have contemporary documents that show how Paul traveled around and preached about this Jesus among his compatriots in a time when eyewitnesses still lived and the Jewish colonies in Greece and Asia Minor had tight relations with Jerusalem. His opponents would not have had any difficulty refuting a displeasing proclamation if it had been built on fantasies. But Paul knew that he spoke about facts that even those opponents knew well. He can also point to "miracles and mighty deeds" of the kind that a modern man is tempted to dismiss as legendary but that he himself had carried out among those to whom he later wrote (2 Cor 12:12).

It is precisely through these letters, where Paul so openly discusses concrete problems in the congregations, that we have a picture of early Christendom that cannot be dismissed as idealization or legendary. While human weaknesses are obvious in these letters, we also receive a colorful picture of the gospel's power to permeate and transform lives in the newly established congregations.

The Question of Authenticity

Ever since biblical criticism was taken up in earnest during the 1800s, the authority of certain Pauline letters has been questioned. The argument that is commonly held to carry the most weight is the linguistic argument. By analysis of the vocabulary of an author and his manner of expression, one can go a long way when it comes to determining whether a questionable text originated from him. Data processing has been used to analyze Paul's letters in this manner.

However, the method has its limitations. If occasionally, an author uses an assistant to write letters or who speaks according to his instructions, the whole project can completely fall apart. And perhaps it is precisely this that accounts for the problem with those congregational letters of Paul that are often regarded to be *deutero Pauline*, by which it is meant that they were written by some disciple of Paul after his death. Namely, it is the letters to Ephesus and Colossae that are considered to be deutero Pauline. But there is good reason to consider these as authentic letters of Paul also. That will be discussed in more detail in the introduction to Ephesians.

In other words, it can be said that the most important letters, the "chief letters"—Romans, First and Second Corinthians, Galatians, Philippians, and Thessalonians (the first letter, anyway)—are commonly regarded as unquestionably authentic along with the little letter to Philemon.

The letters to Timothy and Titus are the most disputed. This issue will be dealt with expressly in the introduction to those respective letters.

The Letters of Paul as God's Word

How have Paul's letters come to be in our Bible? Of course, everyone knew that they were written by a man and sent to certain addressees in particular cities. How could they be perceived as part of the message that God sent out into the world for all people and all times?

In order to understand this, we have to keep in mind the manner in which the apostles were viewed in early Christendom. They were chosen by Christ. They were sent into the world to speak and act on his behalf. In fact the word *apostle* is the Greek translation of a Jewish term that means "an envoy with full power of attorney," "a deputy who would act and speak in his commissioner's place." He who listened to the apostle and received his word, also received Christ Himself (Luke 10:16). Jesus had promised his apostles that he would send them the Spirit of truth, the Spirit who would lead them into the all the truth, because there was so much that Jesus Himself had not been able to say to them while he was with them (John 16:12–13). For this reason, people were convinced that the apostles were led by Christ and fulfilled his work.

This is why it says in the confession of the universal church's faith that we believe in one holy, catholic Church that is *apostolic*—that is, it has been decisively formed once and for all by Christ's apostles, those whom he chose and equipped with his Spirit. Thus the apostolic word is more than a common word of man. Paul could personally see himself as an insignificant "slave of Christ" who made a distinction between Christ's word and his own (1 Cor 7:2). But it is precisely in his absolute dependence on Christ that he shows his capability as an apostle, and an instrument for the works that Christ wanted to have done.

Therefore, according to Christian conviction, Paul's letters belong to the message that God has sent to us men. We see even the events that preserved precisely these letters and caused them to become part of our Bible as a result of God's good governance, and when we read them in our divine service, we ought to say consistently, Hear the word of the Lord through the apostle Paul.

The Epistle to the Romans

Of the letters of Paul, in our Bibles it is the Epistle to the Romans that comes first. As we have seen, this is for purely external reasons. But it is without a doubt that Romans deserves the ranking it has received. Here we receive a summary of the gospel that is more detailed and systematic than in any other letter of Paul. The reason is clear. Here Paul writes to a congregation with which he is personally unfamiliar. And he writes to the capital of the world, from where impulses and new thoughts spread throughout the immense empire. Paul had desired to go there for a long time. With his strategic view, he must have understood what it would mean for the Christian world mission if the gospel could get a firm foot in Rome. When he writes this letter, his travel plans have begun to firm up. He plans to travel to Spain, and on the way there, he will also visit the world's chief city. This is why he sends a letter to the congregation there, a letter in which he presents himself and lays out the gospel that he knows he has received from Christ to preach to the Gentiles. In this manner we receive here a more coherent and complete statement concerning the chief points of the gospel than in any other letter of Paul. The disposition is clear and strictly implemented. Paul does not discuss any local problems and does not need to take issue with any misconduct or misstep as he so often had to do elsewhere. He does not respond to any special conditions that only the recipients know about. For example, if one compares Romans with the Corinthian letters, the differences are immediately noticeable. The Corinthian letters are caused by concrete problems. The contents of those letters answer specific questions and the directives are for special problems. However, the content of Romans is a rather basic investigation of the faith's most important truths. In this sense, it is reminiscent of Ephesians, which for good reason can be assumed to be a type of *shepherd's letter*, a circular letter to the congregations in Asia Minor, and for that reason does not contain any references to local conditions. Yet in both cases, these are real letters written for particular reasons to a particular audience.

When Was Romans Written?

This question can be given a rather exact answer. Paul actually says that he is now planning to travel to Jerusalem with the money he collected in Greece to help the poor in the mother congregation before he comes to Rome (Rom 15:25). We know that he took that trip in the spring of the year 57 (or 58? Here there is an uncertain margin of one year). He spent a few months in Corinth before he departed. Because the greetings in the last chapter of Romans show visible traces of it coming from Corinth, one assumes that Romans was written there. Thus it was likely written during the winter of 56–57, approximately twenty-five years after the death of Jesus.

The Congregation in Rome

We do not know how the congregation in Rome was established. There was a large Jewish colony and it had tight relations with Jerusalem. Among the peoples listed in connection with the miracle of Pentecost, "visitors from Rome" are also mentioned (Acts 2:10). Christianity must have come to Rome quite early given her close relationship with Palestine. Here, as in other locations, the Christians soon met resistance in the synagogues. This resistance seems to have boiled over into riots and the same sort of tumult that we often hear about in Acts. The Roman historian Suetonius states that Caesar Claudius banned the Jews from Rome because they could not cease the perpetual rioting "caused by Chrestus." Because the name of Christ was often confused with the more common Chrestus, it is assumed that the strife Suetonius heard about among the Jews was over whether or not one was for or against Christ. So Suetonius believed that Christ was a party leader among them. In any case, the Jews had to leave Rome. It seems to have happened in the year 49. In Acts (18:2), we read that it was in this context that Aquila and Priscilla came to Corinth and became Paul's closest coworkers there.

When the Jews were banned from Rome, the Gentile Christians were the only ones that remained, and they came to dominate in the congregation there. We also see that Paul counts Rome as among the Gentile Christian congregations, which belonged to his mission field. At the same time, the fact that there must have been a not insignificant Jewish minority permeates the letter. Paul often takes regard for the Jews and their place in the church directly. Apparently, the imperial ban no longer applied. Almost a decade had passed since Claudius, the Caesar who issued the ban, had died and was succeeded by Nero. It was not uncommon in antiquity for a new ruler to mean a new policy.

In his famous forward to Romans, Luther says that this letter is "the true crown of the New Testament and the clearest gospel." There is good reason for this judgment. What salvation through Christ means is described here with a thoroughness and breadth that has no comparison in any other book of the Bible. If Romans sometimes sounds strange or completely shocking to a modern reader, it is because so many live in ignorance of what the gospel really means. All the more reason to read it with careful consideration.

Romans 1

1–7, Heading and Salutation

The very first thing in a letter written at this time was the sender's name. We are accustomed to that coming at the very end. However, the custom of antiquity was more practical. This is plain to everyone who has ever turned a letter over or perhaps searched amid the scribbles in the margins to see from whom it came.

How would Romans have looked if we still had the original?

Certainly, it would have been a roll of papyrus paper, the pages of which were glued edge to edge. The height of the paper would have been about the size of that found in a common [Swedish] school textbook. Altogether, the length of the roll if one unfurled it completely would have been considerable: approximately three and a half meters from one end to the other. One never did this. The text was written on the inside and arranged in narrow columns, somewhat like in a contemporary newspaper. One began reading from the left and rolled up what he had read. Thus one never had more before him than what would correspond to a page in a contemporary book. On the outside of the scroll, there was nothing but the addressee's name.

One always read out loud in antiquity, even if one was alone. What Paul wrote was meant to be heard rather than seen. Sentences that we think are long and difficult take on a completely different life when one listens to them. In my translation, I have attempted to suggest the well-balanced structure of the first long sentences by portioning them up into shorter lines than we normally do in a text of prose.

If we had Romans in our hands now and began to roll it out, the first thing we would encounter, above the very first line in the first column, would be the name of Paul. That which followed would develop a sort of presentation of both Paul and his message. Paul is writing to a congregation that he never personally visited, so he tells them who he is: a servant (or rather a slave, as the word can also be translated) to Jesus, who is the Christ and thus the Messiah of God. From this Christ, Paul has been called to be an apostle. The word *apostle* means "a fully empowered envoy who is appointed to represent his commissioner to speak and act on his behalf." The task that Paul has received is to preach the gospel among the Gentiles.

Paul gives a short summary of this *gospel*. This is not, as we often believe, a common comforting speech about the goodness of God. It is a very particular message. It is already laid down in the Old Testament (the holy scripture), and thus in the word, as a message from God. The gospel deals with God's Son and says something that many in our day would call "dogma" or "theology." The gospel says that Christ is both God and man. One must see Him according to both "the flesh" and "according to the Spirit of holiness" as Paul says with a couple pregnant but hard to translate terms. "According to the flesh" means in the natural, human, historical context in which we men are involved. According to this, Jesus is a Jew, born in Palestine, within a family that could trace its heritage back to the old dynasty. But "according to the Spirit of holiness," he stands in another context, that of the Spirit and the history of salvation where God works to save fallen humanity. And there, God Himself has shown that this Jesus was God's Son, clothed with power like no one else. This He has proven by waking Him from the dead. It was just so with Paul personally. When he encountered the Resurrected One at Damascus, he was convinced that Jesus really was the Messiah, and that God had thus proved this "resurrection from the dead." Paul knows that Christ's resurrection means that there is a day of resurrection coming for all of us. Christ is the first. By Christ's resurrection, God has shown what He is able to do with everyone who believes in Christ. Ever since Easter, it has been clear that there is resurrection from the dead.

Paul has received two things from this Christ: the first is grace, forgiveness, the right to be a child of God, and the second is his commission to be an apostle to the Gentiles.

The Romans are also among the Gentiles to whom he is sent. And now Paul is finally done with this introduction that also serves an explanation for why he, a stranger, writes a letter to "God's beloved in Rome." Thus the name of the addressee follows here: Paul writes to God's "called and holy" in Rome. The name can invoke wonder. The first word says less and the other more than many believers today think that one ought to say about a Christian. To be "called" does not sound so noteworthy and to be "holy" sounds utterly pretentious. But both words say precisely what the New Testament means. One becomes a Christian by God's calling. The disciples did not choose their Master, but they were chosen by Him. That this call must be answered with a yes is true and certain, yet the decisive thing is that one was called, that God willed it. And every Christian is "holy" because he has been set apart as God's own and has had everything forgiven. It is something that depends on God and not on us.

This content-saturated introduction is followed by an equally rich greeting with a desire for grace and peace. What that word means is best shown by the letter that now follows.

8–15, The Reason for the Letter

Paul's custom is to open a letter with a thanksgiving. It is his way of saying something kind: he speaks about why he thanks God for those to whom he writes. In this case, it is actually the simple fact that there is a great and blossoming Christian congregation in the world's capital. People all over the world are talking about it. Yes, Paul literally says it is broadcasted—a custom in this Christian proclamation of one of God's greatest deeds. As so often, Paul says yet again that he constantly prays for his fellow Christians and that he has long prayed that he should come to Rome. He knows that he has a debt to pay. He who was a persecutor has become an apostle and has been sent to the Gentiles. Therefore he has obligations to both "Greek and barbarian." The Greeks were cultured people; the barbarians were subjected people on the edges of the empire or strangers on the other side of the border. We can ponder why Paul has not mentioned the Romans. He certainly did not count them as "barbarians." He himself was both a Roman citizen and a "Greek." His mother tongue was Greek, which was also the official language in the eastern half of the empire. The Christians in Rome spoke Greek. A century would pass before Latin was used as a language of worship. Thus Paul writes in Greek, and his letter certainly did not need to be translated when it was read.

16–17, The Theme of the Letter: Justification by Faith

Once Paul has explained his duty and his willingness to preach the gospel in Rome, he moves on to his office and clarifies what he plans to speak about: the gospel as the message of justification from God that one receives in faith.

He begins by saying that he is not ashamed of this message. He is very well conscious that it is foolishness to the Greeks and an offense to the Jews. But he has been able to see—in his own life and in the lives of countless others—that this message, the gospel, is the power of God for salvation when one receives it in faith.

Here "the righteousness that comes from God" is revealed. In the Greek, it speaks about "God's righteousness." It was precisely these words in just this place that let loose the whole Reformation when they gave Luther clarity concerning the nature of the gospel. As a university lecturer, he taught classes on Romans and spent a lot of time brooding over the meaning of "God's righteousness." Did it mean the righteousness that God demands? This was the common interpretation. It can seem obvious. Within us all, we have a natural sense of what is right. We know that God wants what is right. Thus we believe that the way to God must consist in doing what is right in order to be righteous before God.

Now Luther had two problems with which to wrestle. One was that he had the purely personal experience that he was never successful performing this righteousness that God demanded. The second was that as an expositor of the Bible, he had noticed that Romans was completely unclear when one let righteousness mean the good that we should achieve if we were to be God's children. Then it dawned on him that *God's righteousness* in purely linguistic terms means something different: namely, "a righteousness that comes from God," "something that God gives." With this interpretation, it was suddenly possible to understand Paul. Luther had found the key to the gospel.

18–25, Fallen Humanity Lives under the Wrath of God

God's righteousness is revealed in the gospel. It is revealed in a fallen world for a humanity that has fallen away from God. Paul says there is something else that is also
revealed from heaven, and that is the wrath of God. This wrath is God's eternal and inexorable opposition to everything evil, His jealousy that is an all-devouring fire to that which is impure. This wrath rests upon all mankind who "by their unrighteousness suppress the truth."

In reality, man is created to know God and to be His children. Among all the earthly creatures, man alone has been given the ability to perceive the Invisible. "God's invisible being can be perceived," Paul says with deliberate accentuation. Man has a spiritual eye, an ability to intuitively and spontaneously apprehend with the heart's immediate experience a bit of the reality that is otherwise not available to our outer senses. Man has the ability to perceive the nearness of God and encounter Him "in His work"—in nature and that which happens all around us. Paul says something here that modern research into the history of religion has confirmed: Religion comes about spontaneously, not through a long development. It does not begin with primitive rituals in order to rise from polytheism to monotheism. Neither does it spring from reflections and speculations about the origins of the world, about a first cause or invisible powers behind natural phenomena or some such thing. Instead it is born spontaneously through religious experience, through an encounter with something that man stands before and perceives as a Lord, who has everything in His hand and who desires something with our lives.

Thus there is something "that one can know about God" no matter what people you belong to. We usually call this a common revelation. The law that is written on everyone's heart also belongs to this common revelation, as Paul says in the next chapter. All men ought to be able to know this true God, so that they can "praise and thank him as God." But it has not gone so well. The fall into sin has even garbled this. The enemy of God has put his mark on us. There is something in the nature of man that does not want to "praise and thank him as God," such as He really is. Instead she wants to test, speculate, criticize and determine how God must be if she will accept Him. This is to "suppress the truth with unrighteousness" and not allow God to be who He is. One can only learn to know God by bowing before Him in worship and obedience, in faith and trust. Instead men begin to speculate about God as if our thoughts could be the measure of God's actual being. It is a common corruption of religion; it is just as common in our day as it was in Paul's that one believes he has the right to think what he wants when it comes to God. But when men trust in their own wisdom, knowledge, and judgment and believe that they can use them as a measuring stick for God, they go helplessly astray. Paul has seen this all around him. These Greeks who praise themselves for their wisdom can simultaneously build temples to the ambiguous gods of Olympus and a series of oriental animal figures. It was not without reason that Paul, when he wandered about in Athens "was moved in his spirit, when he saw how filled the city was with idols" (Acts 17:16). Humanity has not taken its knowledge of God seriously but pushed the truth away to make room for a lie. Thus Paul does not mean that one should learn something from the Gentile religions. Without a doubt, there can be traits in them that one can recognize as truly divine knowledge, but it is the mark of human error to think that one would be able to get any real knowledge from them, something that would be able to complete what we know through the revelation of scripture.

26–32, God Punishes the Ungodly by Allowing Them to Go Their Own Way

Thus people have not taken their knowledge of God seriously. They know that he exists, but they have not wanted to seek him in earnest. Instead they have made a religion that suits them better. And God has let them have their way. This is the punishment that has come upon them. To abandon God means to be left to "the spirit that is now at work in the sons of disobedience—" (Eph 2:2 ESV). God's enemy has a lien on man. There is something in our nature "that neither wants nor can bow itself before God's law" (Rom 8:7). Paul calls it "the flesh" or sometimes "the old man." It is this that breaks forth and characterizes one's life unless it is placed under the obedience of God. It can take many different forms, either coarse or more refined. Here Paul gives a very dark picture of how the Gentiles live. It builds upon the daily experience that a Jew would have while living in Hellenistic cities. Naturally, Paul does not mean that everything he lists would occur with every individual Gentile. But he means that all of these things occur among them, that this part of our nature perpetually breaks forth and is seen as something natural. The Gentiles accept it among themselves and regard it as something that exists with others. And this picture of everyday life in antiquity is a picture that one can get from Roman authors such as Petronius and Juvenal, who in large part confirm what Paul says. He who has grown up in a Christian milieu that has been around for a millennia may think the picture is improbable. But the more the secularization of the West shows its consequences on the ideals of life and moral concepts, or lack of moral concepts, the more probable it appears. When the old man is no longer subject to God's discipline, everything begins to break up as we proceed and carry on.

And now Paul says this is God's punishment. One believes that he can go his own way, that he has freed himself and that he lives as he wants. In fact, he bears God's judgment. The judgment rests in the way he is left to the powers he has preferred to God. Three times Paul uses a word with the basic meaning of "left" and with connotations that have been rendered with "given into someone's power," "let something be sacrificed to," "put a price on someone." So the phrase can encompass sexual promiscuity, loose pornography, unrestrained violent crime, and similar phenomena as a sign that God's wrath rests upon a people who has not taken the knowledge of God seriously. And of course, the situation is no less serious if one does not consider it worthwhile to learn the gospel, rather than just settling for the vague knowledge of God, which even the Gentiles can perceive through his work.

Paul explicitly mentions homosexuality because it stood out as particularly shocking for the Jewish people. They knew that it was against God's will. But when they came to live among the Gentiles, they encountered an environment that they never thought possible.

It is completely clear that Paul also means that homosexuality is against God's will. It is a sign that something is irregular in the nature of man. It ought to be noticed that he puts it in line with everything else that is evil and derived from the innate ruin in our nature. This belongs with the crazy desires that can be found among us, in the same manner as greed, envy, contentiousness; the desire to slander, play the bully, and brag; and all the other things that Paul lists here. These drives can be found in different manners and in different degrees with different individuals. But we all have our share of them. They sit in our nature and are innate. Thus Paul does not mean that they are the consequence of personal evil and that we as individuals should have been able to be free of them if we had only desired it. What he describes here is something that happed with mankind. This also applies to homosexuality. It can belong to the inheritance we bear and is part of our old man, that which "by daily contrition and repentance must be drowned and die with all sins and evil lusts" as the catechism says in the chapter on baptism. A Christian can have the homosexual drive, precisely as he can lust after another's possessions or for revenge. But he knows that it is something that he shall not allow free course in his life but crucify instead. He also knows a perfect forgiveness for it and that it does not hinder him from being a child of God. Therefore a homosexual Christian refrains, just like an unmarried Christian, from having an active sex life, and he trusts in God to give him blessings many times over again in his other areas of life, just as Jesus has promised that it shall happen with everyone who for his sake abandons something of that which the world does not want to be without.

Romans 2

1–10, Even the Jews, God's Own People, Live under God's Wrath

Thus Paul has said that the Gentiles are without excuse. Now he continues: Therefore you are without excuse, you who judge (he means you Jews) precisely because you are conscious of how bad it is among the Gentiles and look with disdain upon their moral decay. You know that there is a divine law, but do you yourself keep it?

A Jew could know that he was a sinner. But he could count on still possessing a special status because he belonged to God's people. "Even if we sin, we still belong to you, because we know your power." The Gentiles would be "condemned in wrath," while his own people would be "instructed with gentleness." So we read in "Wisdom," one of the Old Testament's apocryphal books. Such thoughts were so common among the Jews that Paul did not need to say who he was citing or whom he was addressing when he took them up. Do you believe that you shall escape judgment? he asks. Do you believe that God shall have patience with you endlessly? Do you not know that God refrains from judging in order to give you, precisely you, time for repentance? Here you go and gather wrath upon your head. It will catch up to you on the great day of reckoning. Have you not read in the scriptures that God repays everyone according to their deeds?

Then Paul gives a concentrated characterization of the law's way to God. Eternal life is given to those who live according to the law and keep it. And this does not mean merely an outward righteousness. It means to do good and do it with endurance. It means to be oriented toward God, to seek His "glory, honor and immortality"; in other words, seek God and His kingdom with all your heart. And naturally, Paul means that we all fall short here. But there is something else he wants to say in this context: that there is no difference between us men before God's law. The cause of salvation is completely the same. Perhaps, the Jews expect that salvation shall first and foremost come to them because they belong to His people. Right, Paul says, but God's wrath also comes first and foremost to the Jew if he does not keep the law.

We as Christians have every reason to listen attentively when Paul speaks to his own people. According to the New Testament, it is precisely the Christian church that is God's people, the new Israel. This is certainly a matter of a New Testament (covenant) that is not grounded in the law but in Christ. But there are still similarities that make it so we can fall to the same temptations that Paul warns the Jews against here. The type of man that Paul describes here is also found within Christendom. We all have something of it within ourselves. There is the man who has moralistic principles and sees the differences between his way of life and others (which can have good reason) and who for this reason begins to look down upon "the others" and "half unconsciously" counts himself as a better type of person. There is also correspondence about this with those in Christendom who figure that all is in order because they are baptized and have religious interest and a decent life. Or the faithful type who is well conscious that he is a poor sinful man, but who never seriously asks himself about what could and ought to be different and rather takes forgiveness as a self-evident thing. It is altogether an example of this spiritual security that Paul addresses here. What he makes stark and clear is that he who lives in such a manner lives under God's wrath and comes under judgment. And his word is directed at all of us: "You man, every one of you who judges."

11–16, God Makes No Distinction between Peoples

God's law is for all. If we haven't had the law revealed to us within scripture, then in any case, we have the law written upon our hearts.

There is a "common revelation," and the conscience and the sense of right and wrong also belong to that, and this is true of all people. However disoriented and uncertain this understanding can be, one still cannot escape knowing that there are things a man ought to do.

What Paul wants to say is not that every man who follows his conscience comes to God. He brings to mind the conscience and the natural knowledge of right and wrong to show that we are all without excuse. In the day "when God judges the secrets of men," it will come to be shown that no one measures up, neither Gentile nor Jew.

17–24, To Trust in Your Morals Is to Condemn Yourself

When Jews—or let us say "moralists"—mean to belong to the right type of people through the law and their concepts of right and wrong (their ideology or their ideals), then it means that these people condemn themselves. Essentially, it means saying yes to the law. One recognizes that it is right. But then the law shall also apply completely and fully. It is a way to eternal life, but only for the one who fulfills it. And now, here comes Paul with his inquisitive questions: You who hold to this, do you live as you teach? Without mentioning it, Paul apparently has Jesus's own teaching in mind. He assumes that the listeners already know this. Essentially, there was a basic knowledge that was handed down to every Christian, a knowledge that the apostles "received" from Jesus Himself and that consisted of that which they themselves had heard and seen. Paul also assumes in this context that all Christians know what Jesus said in the Sermon on the Mount: that it is already adultery to even look with lust upon another man's wife, just as it is murder to be angry with your brother. He who prides himself on the law is at the same time condemned by the law when it is really applied. Moreover, there were of course moral mistakes among the Jews also, though it did not happen so obviously and shamelessly as among the Gentiles.

What Paul points to when he speaks about "robbing temples" (or "committing sacrilege" as the expression is likewise translated) is not clear. It seems as if some Jews enriched themselves in some manner from the Gentile temple funds without being too careful about the methods and without questioning whether they deserved the money from the idolatry that they denounced.

25–29, The True Circumcision

Circumcision was the sign of the covenant for the Jews, a proof that a man belonged to God's chosen people. Completely right, Paul says, but the covenant demands obedience. If one does not keep the law, then one cannot invoke the covenant. Then one is just like the uncircumcised. The real circumcision is in the heart. It can only happen through the Spirit—through a spiritual renewal.

Romans 3

1–8, God Is Always Right in His Judgment

If the Jews are now subject to the same judgment as the Gentiles, then does not this all become meaningless, what God did when He chose them for Himself? Certainly not, Paul answers. The Jews have received something that no one can take from them. They have received God's word with all these promises. If any of them have fallen into unbelief, then this does not change God's plans. Later on, in chapters 9–11, Paul will come back to this subject. When men doubt, it only serves to show all the more clearly how faithful God is and how He is always true. Before God, all men stand as liars. They have been unfaithful to that which they should have held firm. It is a very good thing that this is clear, Paul says. It is when we recognize our weakness that we may encounter God's faithfulness in earnest. Paul then cites the fifty-first Psalm. (According to the Greek translation, the Septuagint was always used among Jews and was taken over by the early church.) It is this Psalm that we usually use as the confession of sin in the high mass. Paul needs only cite a partial phrase, not even a full sentence. All knew that it was a matter of David's confession, the expression of a crushed heart. And it is precisely there that it says that God is just and true, while I stand there as a sinner during a well-deserved judgment. My sin makes God appear all the more clearly in His majesty.

But then comes a question that Paul certainly heard often. If our sin also serves to exalt God, why shall we then need to be punished for it? Is it not unfair of God? Paul challenges at once and says that one can only ask this if one does not know God but measures Him by human means. That God could have the ability to be unfair is an impossibility. He is the judge of the whole world, He who holds justice in His hand. All justice comes from Him. Justice is that which fits with His will and His being. This, that God can oblige evil even so much as to bring about something good from it, does not excuse the sinner who does the evil. It is here that some of humanity performs the worse misuse of God's goodness. They say that if God finally lets some good come of sin and uses all to the best, and if God's grace overflows as our sin increases (as Paul in fact says in chapter 5), then cannot one sin with a good conscience? Paul has heard the charge. Sometimes it came from his critics, who wish to show how unreasonable it is to say that all depends on grace. And sometimes it has come from those who invoke Paul but have misinterpreted him and "used grace for promiscuity." Paul dismisses them all with the curt warning that they will get their well-deserved judgment. The gospel of God will not be distorted in such a manner.

9–20, The Whole of Humanity Stands under the Righteous Judgment of God

Paul now summarizes everything he has said up to this point. Both Jews and Greeks stand under God's judgment. If someone does not want to believe it, then they ought to listen to what scripture says. Paul cites one Bible passage after another, most of them from the Psalms. All deal with members of God's people and all say the same thing. There is trouble among them. Naturally, just like the moralists of our day, a Jew could say, "In any case, it isn't so bad. There are still good people who honestly do their best." Paul would have answered that more is needed to be righteous before God. Possibly, he would have pointed to the words of Jesus in the Sermon on the Mount: it concerns the secrets of the heart, thus our intents and desires. And then it is true without exception: there is no one righteous.

Yet Paul has another argument at hand for those who want to say, "This doesn't apply to me." That is precisely what it does, he says. The demands of the law apply to everyone who hears them, all those who have received the law and learned to know it. And at the very end, Paul gives a classic formulation of the law's task and says something that has been just as surprising and shocking for people throughout all ages. The usual conception is that the law speaks so that we shall be good and righteous people and in this way come to God. People used to believe that if they seriously obeyed God and listened to Him, then it must mean that they would become better and better. But the result was the opposite. In their own eyes, they were only worse. They would see more and more wrong with themselves. They noticed that there was much more missing than they had anticipated and that the law demands more than they could provide. And this is precisely the purpose, Paul says. Every mouth that has excused himself or bragged about this or that good moral characteristic shall be stopped, and we all shall stand there in our guilt. "For by works of the law, no man is justified before God." Good works of the law are precisely those works that the law demands: first and foremost, love. No one is finished with these deeds. To be righteous means to be finished with all that God demands. And "no flesh" has done this, Paul says, meaning no created being, not a single man. What the law accomplishes is that it lets us see our sin and our guilt before God.

With this, Paul is finished with the first part of the letter. He has set up its theme and explained the problem. Now comes the resolution.

21–26, Justification from God

Paul introduced the section he just concluded with the words, "God's wrath is revealed from heaven . . ." Here he begins the next great section by saying, "But now the righteousness of God has been revealed . . ."

This righteousness that descends from God is also the salvation of humanity's helpless situation. He who receives it "is right as rain."[1]

---

[1] Here Bo Giertz uses a play on words that doesn't translate well. The Swedish word for *righteousness* is *Rättfärdighet*, and so one who is "*färdig med det rätta,*" or "finished with the right," has become right or "finished working to be right." They are, as it were, right as rain.

Here there is no unpaid debt, no unfulfilled demand. Everything is as it should be between us and God. And he has become this "apart from the law," "through faith in Jesus Christ." The law's demand has nothing to do with the righteousness of God. This has been "revealed," just as God reveals that which was hidden from us before, that which only He knew and only He could bring about. So the righteousness of God descends upon "all those who believe." It is received in faith, as a gift and a promise: "There is no difference." Measured by the yardstick of human righteousness, there can be great differences between villainous and decent people. But before God, we are all sinners who have lost the glory, the likeness of God, the sonship that man received in creation. We all carry something that cannot be united with God, something that draws judgment and death upon us. But we can now all be made righteous and be set in a right relationship to God as guiltless children. And it is completely undeserved: "by his grace as a gift."

Then Paul goes so far as to essentially say how this saving righteousness has come into the world. It has happened "through the redemption that comes to us in Christ Jesus." *Redemption* is a word that essentially means "released" or "ransomed" and is usually used when a slave receives his freedom back for a sum of money. Christ has ransomed those who were slaves. God had "put him forward as a propitiation." Means of propitiation have been found in all times. Because man has the ability to experience his guilt before God, there is also a need for reconciliation with God all over the world. God had given Israel the Temple and sacrificial services as such a means of propitiation that should be used "until the time of reformation" (Heb 9:10). Here Paul uses a word for "propitiation" that could also be used for "the mercy seat," the lid with cherub statues that covered the arch where the tablets of the law were kept in the Holy of Holies. It's possible that Paul is pointing to just this "seat of mercy." This was where the high priest sprinkled the blood of atonement for the sins of the people once a year on the great Day of Atonement (Yom Kippur). This mercy seat was kept hidden from the view of the people. No one but the high priest had seen it. But God had placed the mercy seat of God before our eyes so that all could step forth and receive the redemption and the righteousness of God. This is given through "faith in his blood." Faith receives what the blood has accomplished. Christ is the sacrificial lamb. He has died in our place. With His death, He has atoned for our sin.

So God has shown that He is righteous. He cannot compromise with sin. That which is evil can never be one with Him. Therefore neither can we be united with Him. Before Christ, God had as much as suspended His judgment and overlooked sin in expectation of the fullness of time when He would show that He was righteous and at the same time make us sinners righteous. Christ took this sin that could never be united with God to Himself. He who was true God was "made to be sin for us," as Paul says elsewhere (2 Cor 5:21). So God and our sin met. It means a death sentence upon sin. Yet death did not fall upon us but on the Son who died for us. So God has shown that His sentence upon sin stands fast. But at the same time, He has made it possible for us sinners to receive complete forgiveness and stand before Him righteous through faith in Jesus.

27-31, A Righteousness without Works of the Law

Do our good works not count for anything? No, Paul says, in this respect, they don't. They are excluded, "locked out," "prohibited," as one could translate it. This is not according to the normal laws of morality. According to them, there is call for good works. But here the law of faith applies, and it says that all are sinners and are made righteous completely without warrant, without works of the law. Again we must remember that the deeds of the law also include the good deeds of love, the best we can provide. Our virtues have nothing to do in this connection. And it is good. If virtues are to apply, then mistakes and omissions shall also apply, and then we all end up in the red. But God is really a God of salvation for both Jews and Gentiles. His kingdom is not for a small group of morally upstanding people but for the great mass of sinners. He who created them all has a heart for them all. It is precisely for this reason He has made it possible for all to be righteous through faith in Jesus.

But is the law repealed? Does that not let rudeness and irresponsibility loose? No, on the contrary, Paul says. We really make the law apply. Justification happens apart from all good deeds, in the meaning that good deeds neither make nor take from it. But he who has been justified is never without good deeds. They follow from faith. Paul returns to this issue further on in the letter.

Romans 4

1–8, The Old Testament Also Witnesses to the Righteousness of Faith

Paul just said that the righteousness of faith is something that the Law and the Prophets (thus, the Old Testament) also witness to. It is this that he wants to show now.

He begins with Abraham, the great gateway figure in the history of salvation. All Jews looked up to him as their tribal father, proof that they were a chosen people. And now Paul can cite Genesis (15:6), which says that Abraham believed God and that it was this that was counted to him as righteousness. Paul emphasizes the importance of the word *counted*. It means to put something on a person's account. It can be a question of sins that are counted so that one must answer for them. It can also be a matter of God's righteousness—that which is counted to us as righteousness when we believe. This was how Abraham became righteous. Even David speaks about this righteousness, Paul says. He praises the man whose sins God does not count. If one depends on his good works, then one cannot hope in God's righteousness. But if one receives it for nothing, then one is empty when he comes to faith "in him who makes the ungodly righteous." Paul really means what he says here. God justifies the ungodly, not the pious, good, noble, or loveable. Later he comes to show that God lets us all understand that we are "ungodly," and only then can we take and receive that which we receive in Christ.

9-12, The Righteousness of Faith Does Not Depend on Circumcision

But circumcision? Now, for a Jew, this was the sign that a man belonged to God's people. Paul answers by showing that Abraham was already righteous as an uncircumcised man. Afterward, he received circumcision as confirmation. This is why he is now a spiritual father to both the uncircumcised (if they believe) and the circumcised (also with that caveat that they believe).

13-25, Neither Does the Law Give Righteousness, but Only Faith

Neither does "the Righteousness of Faith" depend on the law. Paul has said it before, and now he shows that this agrees with what the scriptures say about Abraham, who received the promise that the whole world should be his inheritance and would be possessed by his descendants. This was a popular belief among the Jews. Though it cannot be directly inferred from the Old Testament, Paul accepts it without hesitation because he knows that Jesus is the Messiah and that everything has been put under Him. He is the fulfillment of the promise that was given to "Abraham and his seed." And this promise was completely independent of the law. Had it been bound to the condition that Abraham's descendants should fulfill the law, the promise would have been worthless. Paul has already shown how the law places all of humanity, even the Jews, under the wrath of judgment. The law does not bring us closer to God. If there wasn't any law, at least then people would not be trespassers who did the opposite of the law's express commandment. Here there is a fatal connection: law → trespass → wrath of judgment. But in contrast to this, ever since the days of Abraham, God has placed a different connection that Paul gathers in the word: promise → faith → grace. The promise was not bound to any condition. This means that Abraham would be a forefather for many people. The promise could seem improbable, as old as Abraham and Sarah were then. But Abraham believed God. And here Paul says something about God that shows how he thinks about the righteousness that comes from faith in Christ the whole time. Abraham believed, against all reason, in the God who makes the dead alive and calls forth those who are not so that they come to be. So God did when He resurrected Christ. And so He does when He gives life to those of us who are spiritually dead. Where we have no righteousness, there He counts to us the righteousness that is not our own. That God is able to make us His children can seem improbable to those who are really able to examine themselves and see their egotism and unholiness. But God can do it. Through Christ, it has been made possible. For Christ's sake, all can be forgiven. It is this promise that faith grabs hold of. And in the same moment, the miracle of grace happens. We stand righteous before God.

Here there is also a parallel between Abraham's faith and ours. That which is said of him has its application for us too. He is "the father of us all." As Christians, we have the right to speak of "our father Abraham." Already in this promise that Abraham received, Christ is present. Abraham's faith was also a faith in "the seed"—Christ, He who would come. For us, it is a faith in the resurrected Christ, in He who died for the sake of our sin and rose again in order to bring to us the righteousness of God.

Romans 5

1–5, The Righteous Have Peace with God

What is it now that follows from justification by faith?

First, we receive peace with God. This does not mean a feeling, but a completely new relationship with God. It is something that has in fact changed: We have received peace with God. Before, we were His enemies. We lived under His wrath. We defied Him or mistrusted Him or tried to use Him for our own purposes. Now we have peace with God. This peace can also be called freedom. The Bible uses the same word in both cases.

We have received this freedom through Christ. He has prepared access for us to the grace in which we now stand. Paul uses the expression that is suited for a kingdom or a temple. It is just a question about God's kingdom that has taken form here on earth in the Church. The same can be said of grace as can be said of freedom: it is not a feeling that I experience but an actual relationship, something that encompasses me and is actually there, apart from any feelings.

Thus we can be "proud and happy" concerning this hope we have. A Christian has certainly learned to feel his sin. He knows how serious it is. Paul has now made it clear, with a trembling seriousness, that we deserve nothing but God's judgment and wrath. But that which completely dominates a Christian presence is this: that we are "proud and happy." Paul uses a word that used to be translated as "boastful." It means a joy that is conscious of the fact that one has received something of incalculable value, a favor, a privilege, something one can count oneself lucky to have. And this privilege is "the hope of God's glory." Paul has now said that none of us have retained this glory we received from God. But now Christ has won it back. We are made to be children of God, and we know that God comes to share His glory with us in eternity.

But not only that, says Paul. We can even be proud and rejoice in our suffering. We know that God changes them into something good when we bear them in faith in Christ. Essentially, they teach us perseverance. The way home to God passes through many hardships, temptations, and persecutions. But these things do not break us. They make us stronger. And precisely because we stand to the test, our hope is solidified—the hope that we all share in Christ's victory when He comes in his glory. This hope is not an illusion. It proceeds from the fact that here and now Christ is powerful to keep us standing in all difficulties.

There is further proof that this hope is not an illusion, Paul says. It is God's love that has been poured out into our hearts. Paul means this literally. God's inconceivable love for those of us who are not worthy has been poured over us and found its way into our hearts as a river of forgiveness. We know that God loves us. His own Spirit has taught us this.

6–11, God's Love for Us Sinners

We have learned to know this love by Christ dying for us while we were still sinners. We had not done the least thing to deserve it. Paul thinks about himself and those to whom he now writes. When Christ died on Golgotha, they were all His enemies or were completely and equally guilty before Him. We can express the same truth by saying that Christ died for us before we were even born. God knew all our sins. But He still loved us. Among men, one can perhaps understand someone sacrificing himself for those he has reason to love. But God shows His love through Christ, who died for the ungodly, the evil people who were His enemies.

And it is for just this reason that we have such a rock-solid hope for salvation. The foundation was laid on Golgotha. We were reconciled with God while we were still His enemies. Christ died for all sins that have ever been committed and will ever be committed. There is no limit to this forgiveness. It is this redemption and forgiveness that we receive in faith when we come to Christ and are justified. This is why, even now, an unworthy sinner can be "proud and joyful in God." He can do nothing but lift his head and rejoice when he realizes what he has. "Thanks be to our Lord Jesus Christ, through whom we have received redemption." God has done this. So He also comes to do all that is now needed to carry us the rest of the way. Here we notice how Paul distinguishes the salvation that has already been won through the atonement on Golgotha, and the salvation that we receive when we believe.

12–21, Adam and Christ, the Two Starting Points of Humanity

Christ also means a new beginning for all of humanity. Paul clarifies it by comparing him with Adam, the forefather of humanity. Here there is a similarity. Both have received a decisive meaning for all descendants. And yet what a dissimilarity! Through Adam, sin came into the world, and through sin came death. This caused a radical change within humanity, something that placed an indelible mark upon our human nature. Instead of a natural love for God and joyful obedience, because of sin we have the similarly natural egotism that looks out for itself first of all. We are born this way, and this "original sin" takes form in "actual sin" in all men. Death comes as an essential consequence. A direct command is not needed, Paul says. The law is first given much later. That which separates us from God is not only the conscious disobedience, such as all moralists envision, but it is actually also the inherent egotism we are born with.

Through Adam's fall, God's enemies also received a lien on human nature, and all humanity came under the condemnation that hangs over sin. But now a new intervention has happened, and it affects man's place before God in a manner that surpasses all that happened in the fall. Time after time, Paul has to admit that the comparison falters. It does not do to compare the work of Christ with anything else, much less Adam and the fall into sin. Through Adam's fall, sin came to rule. Sin "became king," as one could rightly translate it. But the "gift of grace" that Christ gives has made us lords, made us kings, so now we can also lord it over death. When Adam opened himself to sin and believed the serpent more than God, the nature of man was poisoned. All had received a share in the fall and disobedience. But when Christ was obedient unto death and fulfilled all righteousness and at the same time died for the unrighteous, He then made it possible for us unrighteous to receive a share in His righteousness and in this manner become righteous before God.

The law was not given so that we should be able to make ourselves righteous. On the contrary, it was given so that we would be able to see the totality of our unrighteousness. Sin would "be so much greater." So now we are able to receive the infinitely great gift when God lets grace "flood over all banks" and makes it possible for all to be God's children. No one receives this gift if he believes that he is essentially good enough as he is, perhaps with a little improvement here or there. For this reason alone, it would be clear just what an unbridgeable abyss there is between us and God.

As anyone can see, this whole manner of looking at Christ requires the story of the fall to be true. A Christian can read the story of the fall precisely as it stands, or he can figure that in the story of the fall, just as in the story of creation, we have what one calls a "stylized history," where great events are characterized by a few short strokes, reminiscent of a stylized drawing. He can figure that there are symbols being used here—that is, if one takes the word *symbol* in its religious meaning and knows that a symbol is not just a picture but encompasses reality and gives us insight to truth. But one cannot get away from the foundational Christian view that when God made his great intervention into the course of the world and gave rise to the first people, they then received from him the ability to live in unbroken divine communion, in a happy security that we cannot now imagine. It was this divine communion that was destroyed when they fell for the tempter and were dragged into the great rebellion against God.

Romans 6

1–11, We Are Free from Sin through Baptism

But if grace becomes ever greater when sin increases, cannot one then continue to sin? Then the grace will be evermore greater! Paul knows that this question is coming. Surely, he has heard it many times. And he rejects it as unreasonable. If a man asks in this manner, then he has not understood anything of salvation and righteousness from God. It is just this that one cannot do if one comes to faith. One cannot continue to sin as if nothing happened. Something actually happened that is all pervading, something that changes the whole of our situation. We have died to sin. And this happened in baptism.

Essentially, baptism means that we have been united with Christ. We have been "united with him," "grown together with him."[1] We have been incorporated into his body, grafted like branches into his vine. The decisive thing in baptism is something God does, something that cannot be seen or surmised by outward means. It is something that man can believe in and receive because God's word says that it is so.

What is it that happens in baptism?

---

[1] The Greek word here, *sumphutos*, is translated as "united" in the English Standard Version (ESV) Bible. It means "to have grown together," and this meaning is reflected in the Swedish translation.

First, we are baptized into Christ's death and buried with Him. We participate in what happened when Christ died. He died for our sins. He took upon Himself the judgment that rested upon humanity. To be baptized "into Christ Jesus" really means to be brought to Him, into His communion, into a new kingdom and a new life. When we come to Him, we encounter judgment over sin and over our old man. "The old man" is the same thing as "the flesh," the selfish ego, "the sinful body." It is our nature that doesn't come from God. In baptism, it is this old man that is crucified together with Christ. Our sin was there at Golgotha. He bore it, and it brought Him into death. In baptism the death sentence upon the old man is confirmed, that which happened on Golgotha.

But when Christ died, He conquered "through the Father's glory," through the unfathomable divinity of God that sacrificed the Son in order to save sinners. Christ, who bore sin, "died to sin." Sin and death lost their right and power over Him and over all who belong to Him. Sin is really a power, an evil will that crushes and destroys. However, we men believe that sin is a temporary expression of our own free will, something that we can do but also leave alone. In fact, it is a power that rules over man as soon as God does not rule over him. "He who sins, is a slave to sin," Jesus says (John 8:34). It is this slavery that Christ has finally put an end to through His death. When He suffered in our place, He redeemed us (bought our freedom) from the power of death. This freedom is found only where Christ is Lord. Therefore a person receives it by being united with Him. This is what happens in baptism.

But of what does this freedom consist? He who thinks like a moralist believes that freedom from sin must mean the same thing as being free of sin, even moral perfection. He who is free from sin must not have any failures and hardly any evil desires. But this is a matter of a completely different freedom. In order to understand it, we, like Jesus and the whole New Testament, must see sin as a ruler, a tyrant who rules over people when they fall away from God. This tyrant is now set aside. He can continue with his claims, he can tempt and entice, torture and hinder. But he cannot make forgiveness go away, and neither can he pry us from Christ when we live in His kingdom.

Essentially, we are baptized not only into Christ's death but also into life with him. We participate in His resurrection. This does not just mean that we shall rise from the dead sometime in the future as He did on the third day; it means that we already now participate in this new life that He carried out of the grave, this life that can never die because He died to death and condemnation once and for all, and has complete forgiveness with Him. We are baptized to live this life and to "walk in life's new essence" as Paul's words can be translated in verse 4. We belong to Christ, and participate in His life. And Christ has put an end to the right of sin to possess us sinners. Christ who "lives for God," in unbroken communion with God, can bring us sinners into this communion when He becomes our Lord.

So this is how we shall look upon our situation, we who are baptized, Paul says. We no longer stand in service to sin. We have died to that life. The old man, the "body of sin," received his death sentence in baptism. Sin can no longer use it in service to him. Now we live with Christ, for God.

Thus baptism is something that man lives in, something that he applies and uses every day. Baptism isn't "symbolic," nor is it a beautiful ceremony that reminds us of God's goodness, nor is it an act of obedience or confession that one does when one is ready to be saved. Baptism is God's action, something that only God can do. Whether God did this when I was a child or later in life, it is something that I will apply, exercise, and use every day.

12–14, The Baptized Life

Baptism characterizes the Christian's life. Baptism means a judgment upon our old man and to all that is within us that is not of God. But baptism does not mean that all this was removed and gone forever. It remains in our "body of death." There is something in our nature that does not want to have anything to do with God. This "old man" must be fought perpetually. And we *can* fight it when we are given over to Christ. But we must know who we will serve: sin or Christ. Therefore Paul says, Let not sin rule in your body of death. Put yourself at God's disposal. You were baptized to this. You have now awakened to new life, you who were dead in sin. Sin shall no longer rule over you. And then there follows a remarkable motivation: you do not stand under the law but under grace. This is inconceivable for the moralist who believes the way to God is through deeds. For him, the law is a means to escape the lordship of sin. He believes that it is precisely by taking the law upon oneself that one can quit sinning. Paul says the opposite: if we stand under the law, then sin rules over us. We are and remain sinners if we shall be measured by the measuring stick of the law. Sin only becomes worse, more intensive, if we try to make ourselves holy and righteous before God with the help of the law.

15–23, Free from Sin in Order to Serve God

That sounds highly precarious for all who sit firmly in the piety of the law. Paul knows this, and again he takes up the constant charge, "Then you can just as easily sin!" In order to show how unreasonable the argument is, he makes it clear that sin really is a power that rules over a man in the same way slave owners from that period would rule over their slaves. Paul appeals to everyday experience. In his day, anyone could become a slave if things went bad for him. He could give himself into slavery, perhaps to escape his debts or just to be fed. But then he was also secure. And so we men have also been secure since we put our lot in with God's enemies and lost our childship with God. No man can be his own lord. We stand in the midst of a fight between good and evil, where one must be on one side or another. Either one has sin as his lord, which will lead to death, or one is subject to "obedience." We expect Paul to say "God." That is precisely what he means, but he is so taken up by the thought that this means a new relationship of obedience to a new Lord that he chooses to say "obedience."

Then Paul uses the picture of a slave who switches lords. Before we were slaves under Sin. (One could very well write the word with a capital letter to show that it is the matter of a personal power.) But we have been redeemed from this slavery. Sin, who really has claim on us, guilty as we are, has been forced to set us free. But he would immediately seize us again, if the Lord who freed us had not at the same time taken us into His service. Now we are His own. We are His slaves, Paul says. He knows that the picture is lacking and he emphasizes that he uses it only in an attempt to sort out the matter for those who are prisoners in the usual human performances. Of course, the problem with the picture is that a slave who switches owners can have it just as wretchedly and be just as unwilling as before. But to be a slave of Christ means to be an heir and child of God. Paul discusses this matter elsewhere in Romans. Here he uses it to make it completely clear that a Christian is free from sin but not free to do whatever he wants. He is free to live under God's power as God's servant. One cannot be free from sin if one does not have all of his debt canceled. And this can only happen through faith in Christ, the faith that makes us righteous. But it is precisely in this faith that we are united with Christ, grown together with Him, as Paul just said. Thus there is no freedom from sin other than for those who belong to Christ. And if one does that then one is "obedient from the heart." This is a different obedience than that which is found in the piety of the law. When one stands under the law, one can be obedient from fear, out of respect for what is right, due to ambition, or because of the desire to be saved or blessed. But here it is a matter of an obedience that depends on the love of the Lord, from which one receives everything and through which one has a desire to serve from the heart. Paul calls it an obedience "from the heart to the standard of teaching to which you were committed" (that it would embody your life). Naturally, this "teaching" is the gospel of Christ, who died for us. Paul does not say that the teaching is entrusted to us. No, it is we who are "given over," "entrusted" to it. It is a creative power, a living word that has put its hand upon us. We have not chosen Christ, but He has chosen us.

Here it is also a question of two different lords and two different services. There is no third. And Paul needs only reference the experience of his audience to show this infinite difference. Now they are ashamed of the service they offered before. They know that it brought them to destruction. The reward that Sin gives to his servants is death. But God gives something completely different. Paul doesn't call it a reward but an undeserved gift, a gift given through grace. This gift is eternal life and it is given "through Jesus Christ, our Lord." Everything depends on Him, and therefore Paul finishes here with these words, just as in other chief passages from the letter (Rom 5:21, 7:25, 8:39).

Romans 7

1–6, Thus We Have Died to the Law

The profound thing that happens when one is incorporated (embodied) into Christ is that not only one dies to sin in order to live for God. One also *dies to the law*. This also happens by dying with Christ in baptism. This death has the same effect as physical death, Paul says. The law ceases to apply when death intervenes. The law binds a wife to her man. But death puts an end to those bonds; the law no longer has anything to say. It is the same way with you, Paul says. And his wording shows that here he clearly sees a parallel to what he described in the former chapter. There he spoke about how we die to sin. Here it applies to the law. He uses a stronger word and says, "You have died to the law." This happened by "being incorporated into Christ's body." Paul means that because Christ bore our sins and died for them on the cross and because we were incorporated into Him in baptism, we became members of a body that died for us. Therefore we have translated His thought with the words "being incorporated into Christ's body."[1] When Paul continues, "So that you may belong to another," it is yet again the same thought as in the previous chapter: we die to the old in order to belong to God and serve Him. This means that we should grow together with Christ through a similar

---

[1] A more wooden translation of the words to which Bo Giertz refers would be "through Christ's body," as the ESV renders them.

resurrection. Here it means that we belong to He who rose from the dead so that we may now "bear fruit to God." It means that our lives will finally be able to be formed to give the result that God had in mind. It is also apparent that Paul means that the law does not lead to this result. Here it is a matter not of following the law with new earnestness and better success but of a completely new way of life. Before, we followed our depraved nature (Paul says "flesh") and we "bore fruit to death." The law only made the matter worse. But now the law no longer applies because we died. It can no longer maintain that we are obligated to die for the sake of our sins. It no longer decides if we can be children of God or not. Now we are members of Christ and live a completely new life. Paul uses the expression "we serve in the newness of the Spirit."[2] It is a parallel to the corresponding expression in the previous chapter (Rom 6:4), where it says that we "walk in the newness of life." In both cases it means a new manner of life where the driving force is life from Christ and the Holy Spirit. Paul contrasts this expression, "newness," with two words that literally mean "written oldness." He means that the old way of life that was characterized by the "written code." And thereby Paul means the law's demand to live perfectly in accordance with it as a condition for salvation. He means the usual moralistic conception that the Bible is a law book with all these paragraphs that specify the conditions for salvation. One misunderstands him completely if one believes that he means the law's literal meaning, so that the new way of life should be a "freer" manner of understanding the law's conditions, while still allowing them to be signposts to God. Christ has not softened the law so that it is easier to come to God in the manner of the law. He has opened a completely different path for us.

7–13, Sin Became Worse through the Law

If the law is something that we need to be free from, then it sounds as if the law is something evil. But this is a thought that Paul is careful to steer clear of. The law is good. It expresses the will of God. But

---

[2] The ESV translates this "the new way of the Spirit," but it literally says "in the newness of the Spirit," as Bo Giertz has translated it here.

when it encounters us fallen men, it cannot help us. On the contrary, it makes the matter worse. It shows us that sin sits much deeper than we thought. It says that we should not even desire evil. But that is precisely what we do. And when we begin to seriously fight against all sorts of covetousness, to put an end to them with the help of the law, they only become more alive. The result is death. We remain under the judgment of death. We find that we do not have the life we ought to have in order to be children of God. And we cannot attain it. It is hopeless. And all this is because of sin. Just when we encounter the law, it is revealed how evil and ruinous it really is.

Here Paul says "I" and the simplest explanation is that he speaks of his own experience. He experienced this as a strict Pharisee. As a child, up until the age of twelve, he had not been obligated to keep the law. Perhaps, in later years he had lived in the faith that outer obedience was enough. But when his understanding of the law deepened and he put all his strength into really keeping it so completely that he would not even covet evil, then it was revealed to him that it did not make him holy, pure, and good but on the contrary drew forth his evil covetousness and condemned him to death.

14–25, The Indwelling Sin

Paul continues to say "I," but now he transitions to speaking in the present tense, about something that is happening now and applies to this hour. This has awakened interest, and it has been asked if what Paul speaks about must not apply to the time before his conversion. This much is obvious: Paul means that what he says here applies to both himself and us others. He doesn't describe a private problem, but a common one. But who is it that he speaks of? The converted or the unconverted?

Paul himself gives the answer in the comprehensive conclusion: "So then, I myself. . . ." He describes us Christians as we are in ourselves, as if we don't have access to that which Christ has done for us. It is not an impious man who he describes. On the contrary, it is a man who from his heart wants to do God's will, who has joy in the law of God and who has "an inner man"—an expression that Paul otherwise uses for the new man, he who grows in strength by the Spirit (Eph 3:16) and who is renewed day by day even as our outward man passes away (2 Cor 4:16). What he describes is the painful experience that a man can have when he really wants to "be a serious Christian" in the conviction that he must root out all evil even within the heart. Then it shows that there is actually something in our own nature that will not be uprooted. One can more or less control the outer deeds, but one cannot change his corrupted nature. When Paul says that "the evil that I would not, that I do," he is hardly thinking about such things as theft, consciously lying, or reviling and dishonest affairs. A Christian does not do such things, and they who do them shall not inherit the kingdom of God. Paul says this rather sharply in many places. But here it means such things as envy, thinking ill of other men, feeling schadenfreude or the desire to give as good as one has got, and being disappointed when one is not praised. No matter how much one despises this, it is still there. This is because of "the law of sin that dwells within my members." Paul also has other names for the same thing: flesh, the old man, body of sin. Because this exists of itself in my nature, I am "sold under sin," a harsh lord who keeps me in his grip. In the preceding chapter, Paul described how I have been redeemed by Christ and received a new Lord. Sin shall no longer rule over me. But it remains in my nature, and therefore, whenever I want to do good, I have to fight. There is always something that hinders me. Paul says in Galatians (5:17): "For the desires of the flesh are against the Spirit, and the desires of the Spirit are against the flesh, for these are opposed to each other, to keep you from doing the things you want to do." Therefore our works will never be perfect as they are in themselves either. There is always some trace remaining of the flesh's opposition, something that is not as we want. Even with a Christian, there is something that will not obey God. Even if one says no to it, opposes it, and steers away from it, there is still something that really hinders it. A Christian can say, "This is not me. I want to say no to this." Still it is there as part of his nature and himself. "Such is who I am in and of myself." I am helplessly lost. But now there is something outside of myself, something Christ does that changes the whole situation.

The picture of a Christian that Paul gives in this section is not a complete picture. Notice that Paul says, "For I know that nothing good dwells within me, that is, in my flesh." This is the picture a Christian "such as I am in myself." But here there is something still more important. There is something outside myself that saves me: the Lord who has died for me. With His Spirit, he can take up residence with in me and then I can obviously say that there is something good in me.

Paul finishes with a cry of distress and a thank you. "Wretched man that I am! Who will deliver me from this body of death?" Paul knows that there is a way out—only one: through Jesus Christ. The final liberation doesn't come before death. So long as life continues, I may continue the fight with my old man. But it already continues on the new terms, thanks be to Christ. Paul now transitions to that theme.

Romans 8

1–11, Life in the Spirit

Paul concludes, "There is, therefore no longer any condemnation for them who are in Christ Jesus." This condemnation that hung over us is suspended and will never manage to fall upon us. This is completely and wholly because of what Christ has done. We may believe and receive. To believe means to come to Christ and be united with him. Then one is "in Christ Jesus," and then "the law of sin and death" has expired. It is this law that says, "He who sins shall die." It has been suspended by "the law of the Spirit of life." This is the new order: we do not need to die because the Spirit "gives life" (2 Cor 3:6). He creates faith in Christ. His law says, He who believes in the Son shall not perish.

So the impossible has become possible. The law could not make us into children of God. It stood powerless before our depraved nature, our "flesh," which could never be changed and freed of sin. For this reason, God intervened. He sent his Son in human form, like us, exposed to the same temptations, the same suffering and death, but without sin. He did it in order to overcome sin and atone for it. Only now did God judge sin, which he had long passed over in his divine forbearance (3:25). But now it was Christ who bore it. In him, it received its judgment, "in the flesh," Paul says. This means that Christ bore our sins "in his body" (1 Pet 2:24). It can also mean that it was the sin in our flesh that now received its judgment.

Only in this manner could the good that the law pointed to be completed. It was completed in us, not by us. We were justified. We became children of God and received his Spirit. Therefore our life has received a complete realignment. We "walk according to the Spirit," as Paul actually says. This means that we are driven and guided by the Spirit on our path through life. The flesh still remains in us. It tries to hinder us in every way it can (Gal 5:17). But here there is yet one decisive difference. Some allow the flesh to rule. They are aligned to that which the flesh wants. One can also translate it "they join the party of the flesh, and take the side of flesh." If one does that, then one is under the law of sin and death. But a Christian allows the Spirit to rule. He puts himself on the side of the Spirit in the fight that is fought within him. Even within him, there is something that neither can nor wants to obey God. It is condemned to death on the cross. This sentence is confirmed in baptism. A Christian confirms it every day. He says no to that which the flesh wants. He knows that this means death, just as he knows what the Spirit wants: life and peace. This attitude is found where the Spirit is found. It is the consequence of a man living in faith in Christ and in communion with him.

So in a certain manner, a Christian is a double being. He is, as Luther says, "Simultaneously saint and sinner." He has a human nature that is marked by sin. For this reason the body must die. But at the same time, he is pardoned and justified. A new life has been kindled within him. He possesses it through the Spirit and in his spirit (the text can be read both ways). It is a life that death does not rule over "for the sake of righteousness"—that is, because Christ died for us and gave us participation in His righteousness. This communion with Christ that we possess in the Spirit means that we too shall be awakened and made alive in the same manner that Jesus was awakened. Thus death and resurrection do not mean that the spirit "is freed" from the body but that our spirits have a new body, a new concrete existence in which we are essentially free from "the law of sin in our members."

12–17, We Are God's Children

God's children are those who "are driven by God's Spirit." God's children also have their flesh remaining. It comes with its demand. But we do not remain in the guilt of it. We have no obligation to it. We don't need to think, "Because this is still in me, it is then hopeless." It can never be hopeless when we have Christ. Because we put ourselves at the side of the Spirit "put the deeds of the body to death"—"the body" here means "the flesh." These are the desires and notions that we say no to. We do this with the Spirit's help. And take notice: it is not a matter of a spirit of slavery, as one who says, "It is so bad but I have to do it." This spirit makes us fearful before God so that we serve as unwilling servants. But here it is a question of the Spirit of childship, he who can say, like Jesus Himself, "Abba Father." The certainty that we have of being children and living under the eye of a good father is a far better motivator than any law can be. And the Spirit also gives us certainty that we are God's children. Paul points to one of faith's deepest experiences, a comfortable inner certainty of childship. Thereby we are also heirs to all this that Christ has won for us: God's kingdom and all the coming glory. But this childship does not mean that we escape suffering in this world. It means that even suffering receives meaning.

18–25, Hope and Suffering

In the New Testament, suffering is a fact. It almost goes without saying, not the least for a Christian who encounters all the enmity that the world spontaneously feels before Christ. But this suffering feels as light as a feather compared to the glory that comes to be revealed "in us," as Paul says—that is, so that we are changed by it. Paul thinks of the day when Christ comes again and makes all things new. Then we shall "together with him step forward in glory" (Col 3:4). We are not the only ones who long after that day. This means all of creation, Paul says. Today the creation is no longer such as it was when it proceeded from God's hand. It has been "placed under corruption." Even here the forces of destruction are effective. This is a consequence of the fall into sin, and it has happened "through the work of another." Here Paul means through the fall of Adam, and because the earth was cursed for his sake (1 Mos 3:17). But already at that time, God had resolved to establish His creation, both man and the world. Therefore God will create a new heavens and a new earth "where righteousness lives" (2 Pet 3:13). It is to this day that creation longingly reaches. We know, Paul says, that the creation groans and agonizes under corruption. We do not know this naturally from our own study of nature—it is a knowledge that only God can give, when through His word He allows us to see the hidden context of existence.

But it is not only nature that groans under the pressure of evil in the world. We Christians do too, Paul says. We do this even though we are God's children and have received the "first fruits of the Spirit." The first fruits were the first of the harvest. They were brought forward as an offering to God. There they were laid upon the altar where it was proof that the fields were now ripe. So the Spirit is the first of the harvest of the kingdom of God that is ripe. We still do not see the harvest, but the Spirit shows that it is there. God's kingdom is near. But "It is so in this hope that we are saved." We are really saved, but it is also something that we hope in. Our childship is not something visible, not a concrete reality, until that day when Christ comes in His kingdom. On this day, our body shall be redeemed. We shall not be redeemed from the body. On the contrary, the body is caught up in salvation. It shall really be freed from the "law of sin" that lives in our members.

26–27, The Spirit That Intercedes for Us

It is not only the creation and ourselves that moan. The Spirit that dwells within us also does this. Even within a man who believes and who prays, there is weakness. It is in this relationship to God, in the life of prayer—so long as it depends on us. But the Spirit comes "to help our weakness." He steps in for us as our intercessor with God. This He does with groaning that we do not understand. Perhaps Paul means that speaking in tongues was an expression for the Spirit's manner of "interceding for us." In any case, He will say that in the end the decisive thing is not the strength and depth of our prayers, but the Spirit Himself. The Comforter and Advocate takes on our cause. Something happens in the hidden depths of our hearts, in the midst of our weakness, a work that God Himself carries out for those who believe.

28–30, God Works Here

Here everything works together—even suffering!—to the best "for them who love God." To love God is not something meritorious; it is not a praiseworthy work that God rewards by letting everything turn out successfully for us. But it is evidence that one lives in the love of God and is drawn into His work of salvation. God carries this through despite all obstacles. A man can certainly say no, though God wants all to be saved. God even calls those who end up saying no. On the one hand, God knows who will answer yes. God "foreknew them." Here Paul uses an important expression that is difficult to translate. It turns up again in other contexts where he speaks about us "being known by God" (1 Cor 8:3, 13:12; Gal 4:9). This is one of the deepest expressions for God's relationship with us. God has felt for us and has taken us into His thoughts and confidence. He knows us, and He still loves us. The word also says this: that God already in the beginning—before the foundation of the world! (Eph 1:4f.)—knew their names and wrote them in the book of life. He now calls them too; they are made righteous and they receive His glory, already now in the hope (so that we can rejoice in the hope of his glory [Rom 5:2]), and finally so that it can be seen with the eyes. Thus all the work of salvation is God's from beginning to end. We can only receive or refuse to do so.

31–39, Therefore We Are Secure

This conviction concerning election inspires a deep security. This too does not depend on us but upon God. Now that He has intervened this way in our lives, we know that He will carry us still further. Who can hinder it? Who can accuse us or condemn us? Previously, Paul very emphatically said that the law, God's own good law, both accuses and condemns us. He knows how many witnesses can stand against us. But here they must all be silent. Christ has died for us. He makes intercession for us. God has declared us righteous in Christ. Now we belong to Him. And nothing can separate us from this love, not even all the suffering that remains, frightful and torturous. Through Christ, we win a glorious victory over all of them. Paul is perpetually piling up new terms: *tribulation*, *distress*, *persecutions*, and *evil powers*. And then he strikes a dash through all of them. They can never separate us from this love of God that we encounter in the gospel. And then Paul finishes, for the fourth time, with these words featuring everything that he wants to say: "in Christ Jesus our Lord."

Romans 9

1–5, Paul Mourns for His People

Paul has spoken of God's election and how God carries it out. But how does this fit with reality? Had God not called Israel? Precisely this Israel that refused to receive the gospel? This is the question that Paul takes up now.

He begins by testifying to his deep solidarity with the people among whom God had allowed him to be born. Should he not love the people who God had loved and chosen? He goes so far as to say that he would have himself condemned if it would save his compatriots. It may sound like an exaggeration, but Paul asserts that it isn't. He could point to Moses as a model. When Israel had fallen and the people had made themselves a golden calf, it was Moses who prayed that God would forgive His people or also blot out his own name from His book. Paul recounts all of the privileges that God has given His people. They are His children; to them belongs God's glory that filled the tabernacle in the desert and overshadowed the Temple. God had made His covenant with them. They had received His law. They were entrusted with the worship of the Temple. They possessed all the promises of the Messiah. To them belonged the patriarchs, and most of all, Christ was born to them, He who had received the name above all names (God's own name!), He who is true God.

6–9, To Whom Belong the Promises?

Thus Israel had received the promises. But then had God kept them? Yes, says Paul, but the promises applied to those who believed. There is a true Israel, a people of the promise, that consists of all those who believe the word of promise, even the gospel of Christ. It is not a natural lineage from Abraham that makes a person a child of God. It is faith in the promise that God gave the fathers. Therefore it is the church that is the Israel of God today (Gal 6:16).

10–18, God Has Mercy on Whom He Will

Now Paul comes to something that belongs to the profoundest of his life experiences: if a man is saved, then it is completely due to God's mercy. Of oneself, one has done nothing to deserve it. One could just as well have been lost. God's decision stands behind salvation, an election of God. Paul said it in the previous chapter, and he develops it here in a manner that awakens the concerns of many people. Can it be determined from eternity that I shall be lost?

In order to understand Paul rightly, one must first remind himself of what he developed with such emphasis in the first three chapters: No man deserves anything but to be rejected. All are under the wrath of God. It is always man's fault if he is lost. Further, one must remember what Paul has also said (1 Tim 2:4): God wants all men to be saved. Concerning the question of Israel, he says further on (Rom 11) that behind God's judgment over those who have fallen lies His plan that in the end all of Israel shall be saved. God's will to save is the first and the last.

But aside from all this, Paul argues very sharply that God is absolutely sovereign. No man can come with any pretense. No one can prescribe what God should will or do. If I am saved, then it has its basis in a completely undeserved grace, a decision of God that I have not merited. God just as well could have left me to the fate I deserved. Augustine and Luther, as well as many others who are regarded as great men in the history of the church, have said the same in similarly pointed form. We stand here before one side of the truth that cannot be conceptually stitched together with the other side of the truth without leaving gaps in the joint. On the one side, there is the truth that it is God alone who saves and that all depends on His will (even His election). On the other side, it is just as true that salvation does not happen automatically but that I am embroiled in a drama where I play a role that I am responsible for. Paul says it, even in this context, a little further on: the fallen man does not need to hold fast to his unbelief. Even the elect must hold fast to the goodness of God, and so on.

When Paul wants to show how God operates in His sovereignty, He uses the example of Jacob and Esau. This example immediately awakens the question: can God be unjust? Paul does not answer the question. This would necessitate that he begin to defend God, and this would be blasphemy. Instead he rejects the question as absurd. That God is just is obvious. It belongs to His very being. For exactly this reason, we do not question why He does what He does. God Himself determines upon whom He will have mercy. This He does for reasons that we cannot see into and shall not question. We shall only note that there is nothing in us that we can point to as reason for God's dealings. God's election does not depend on our will or effort or some other virtue that we think we have. Like Pharaoh, one can have achieved the height of human success. This does not show that one has good standing in the books of God. On the contrary, it can be part of God's judgment—there to show His power. We cannot conceive the reasons that some come to believe while God lets others be hardened. God alone knows the reasons, and they are completely hidden from us.

19-29, We Cannot Make Any Claims against God

Paul takes up an objection that apparently he was accustomed to hearing and that comes up again even today as soon as God's election is spoken of: "But then how can God judge us? Everything depends on Him!" Paul immediately shows that there actually is something that depends on us. But he doesn't say it here. He only rejects the question. We men cannot debate with God. If we begin to criticize God's dealings, then God is no longer our God. He who believes knows that God is always right and always does the best. Only he who is embroiled in rebellion against God can question what God does. If one believes, then one accepts that one is created such as he is. That there are "vessels of wrath," one accepts as a fact. "Vessel" is used in the Bible as a picture of men or people. The man, the vessel, can be filled by God's wrath or by God's mercy. Whichever will occur depends on God, and we cannot demand the ability to know why He does what He does. We do not stand in such a relationship to God that we can negotiate or make demands. All attempts in this war depend on placing man at God's side as an equal. This was the devil's temptation, the original sin: to will to be like God and be able to dispute with Him about what is right and wrong. Faith satisfies itself knowing that God has His reasons. Faith sees God's glory and love glimmer, where unbelief only protests. Paul gives a pair of examples: Faith does not marvel that there are in fact "vessels of wrath"; rather it is amazed by God's patience with them. And it is amazed that God can reveal the glory of His kingdom to others who certainly could not ask for it—for example, Paul himself and those to whom he now writes!

In our Lutheran confessional writings, the question of predestination is handled quite extensively. There it is posited that one must distinguish between that which God knows from eternity and that which he desires from eternity. God desires that all men shall be saved. He knows that some come to receive His salvation, while others reject it. This, His "foreknowledge," is not the cause of evil, nor of sin, nor that some people do wrong. God has not predetermined some to unblessedness. He calls all and offers salvation to us all, and He means it seriously. The "chosen" are those of whom God knows who come to be saved. To them applies "God's eternal election." About them God has determined that nothing shall snatch them from out of His hands. In this meaning, there is a predestination. But only to blessedness.

One must see all these questions in the right context. Luther says that one shall follow the order found in Romans itself. First, one shall concern himself with sin and Christ. When one understands what we possess in Christ, then one shall learn to fight against sin. When one then succumbs to *anfechtung* ("despair"—cross and suffering, such as is described in the eighth chapter) then one can go further to the ninth, tenth, and eleventh to learn "how comforting election is." It is really this that is the key to all talk about God's eternal election of grace: we shall learn to comfort ourselves in that God wants our salvation and that it all depends on Him.

Paul finishes this passage by giving an answer to the question about God's word coming to nothing by the apostasy of the Jews (verse 6). On the contrary, he says it is precisely that which God has said that is now fulfilled. The salvation has come to those who were not of God's people, while only a remnant of Israel has been saved just as God said through the prophets.

Romans 10

9:30–10:3, Why Have the Jews Rejected Their Messiah?

So something strange has happened: the chosen people stand outside God's kingdom, yet the Gentiles have flooded in. This is because God's greatest gift very easily becomes a stumbling block. There is an ambition within us that wants to earn God's grace. It is quite in order for one to try to keep God's commandments with all their heart and "burn with zeal for God," but there is a danger when one wants to be God's child on his own terms rather than God's. It is not without reason that our fathers counted self-righteousness as one of the greatest hindrances to salvation. It is a form of pride and self-assertion that causes a man to not want grace—at least not unless he can persuade himself that he has done something to deserve it. This form of self-assertion can pop up everywhere. It is not only among the Jews that Paul encounters it. The Letter to the Galatians shows how relentlessly he exposes and condemns all attempts to go down this path. Now he takes the opportunity here to show how important it is to have a true insight into just these questions, which men so often dismiss as theological hairsplitting. Those who do this are most often committed to an obvious doctrine of works and take it for granted that one must be able to come to God if one only "does his best." Paul shows us that this is *not* at all quite so certain by pointing to the great tragedy among God's own people.

4–13, The Path of Salvation Is No Longer Law, but Christ

In Christ, the law has received its end—namely, as the path to salvation. In fact, it has never been able to give salvation. No one was able to fulfill it. Its basic condition said, "Do this and you will live." But the gospel, which deals with righteousness by faith, does not say this. To show this change that happens through Christ, Paul uses a well-known word from Moses (Deut 30:11ff.). In writing about this passage, he gives it new meaning in order to clarify what this new path of salvation is. Moses had spoken concerning the commandments and reminded Israel what a privilege and what a responsibility it was to have them—not far off, not in heaven, not in some foreign land, but "very close to your mouth and in your heart, so that you may do it." Paul knows that now the era of the commandments has passed. Instead Christ has come. And now one can say something similar concerning Him. One does not need to retrieve Him from heaven, nor bring Him up from the dead. He is much nearer in the Word, in the gospel. He lays this word in our mouth and in our hearts. Paul emphasizes the words *mouth* and *heart* and repeats them three times because they say something essential concerning faith. By faith, Christ lives in our hearts, and if He lives there, so one confesses His name before the world. There is no real difference between the heart's faith and the mouth's confession. Both express that we have been reached by the gospel and received Christ. Neither does Paul mean by the confession of the mouth the type that we call "a confession of the lips," nor some habitual or conventional confession that does not correspond to the faith of the heart.

Thus the confession of the heart says: "Jesus is LORD." This is the Christian confession of faith in its shortest form, just as we encounter it elsewhere in the New Testament. Jesus has received the name that is above all names. God's own name: "The LORD." The man Jesus is true God. Paul mentions as the saving faith of the heart "that God has raised him from the dead." This does not mean that one is saved by the purely intellectual conviction that just this precise point of the confession of faith is true, but it means that one lives in the communion of the heart with the Risen One and has Him as a living Lord.

This new way of salvation applies to everyone, both Jews and Gentiles. It no longer says "keep the commandments," but "believe in Jesus." Everyone who calls upon the name of the Lord is saved. And the Lord is Jesus Christ.

14–17, Faith Comes through Preaching

But if one should be able to call on Jesus as their Savior, then one must have help in order to believe in Him. Therefore the gospel must be preached. And so that the gospel should be preached, messengers must be sent out. When Paul speaks about "sending out messengers," he uses the verb that corresponds to the word *apostle* and the same word that we have in *gospel* lies in the expression "those who come with the joyous news." He also reminds us that Christ has sent out apostles with his gospel. Christ has established a church and there the gospel shall be preached. Faith arises from this preaching. Thus the proclamation and the divine service are also important. And it is just as important that the proclamation actually puts forth Christ's word, and does not allow the gospel to be formed by the desires of the audience.

18–21, Has the Message Reached?

Could Israel possibly excuse itself saying that it was never able to hear the gospel? In no way, Paul says. God ensures that his message goes out. Paul cites a verse from the Psalms that deals with how the heavens proclaim God's glory. He means that in the same manner, the gospel has gone throughout the world. And then, of course, Israel must have heard it—Israel that stands in the center of the events! But if now Israel has not understood the message? Paul answers that, in any case, that is something rather incredible when considering that even the Gentiles have understood it! This incomprehensible blindness and inability to understand is indicated already in the Old Testament, Paul says. He takes a word that speaks about how God spoke in vain to His people and therefore turned to the Gentiles, who receive his gifts to the envy and resentment of Israel.

Romans 11

1–12, Israel Has Not Been Rejected

Now it can seem as if God rejected Israel. The promise applied to those who believed, and Israel has not desired to believe. Does this mean that Israel has been excluded from God's plans?

Paul answers no. Israel still has a task in the great drama of salvation. God has not forsaken His people. That God is faithful and wants to save His people is still true and shows itself in three ways.

First, it shows in that there is still a remnant of Israel, a faithful core, the true people of God. Paul points to himself. He thinks about the apostles and all the Jewish Christians that are the core in the church. They are the true Israel. By being united with them, the Gentiles are now God's people. It has happened so that the true Israel looks like a disappearing little minority. So it was in the time of Elijah. But this remnant was born by the promise of God and the future hope.

Second, Paul says that God has a good purpose for the Jews when He makes the Gentiles His people. He wants "to incite Israel to jealousy." Paul returns to this thought three times. It is Israel's God and Israel's Messiah who the other people now call upon and receive blessings from. This must be able to open the eyes of the Jews, who have a right to it most of all, if they will only receive it.

Third, Paul points to a mystery, a final goal in God's plan that is still hidden but that comes to be revealed: in the end, all of Israel will be saved, and in that day, the blessing of Christ will come to flood over all the other people in a manner that they had never conceived of. Paul returns to this thought. Here he only suggests. When he speaks about Jewish "failure," he uses a word that means "to give in," "to be defeated," or "to disappoint." Because the failure means that the people are scattered (so that only a remnant remains), as a contrast, Paul can use the expression "full inclusion"[1]—they shall all come back.

Behind this fact, that a remnant of Israel has been faithful, Paul sees God's election. Of course, he himself is proof that everything depends on the mercy of God. He has experienced something that he in no way deserved. But Paul also sees God's operation behind the hardening of Israel. It is God's judgment. The scriptures witness to it, Paul says, and he cites the Old Testament in a typical manner. What God has said in former times also applies to us today. What God said about His recalcitrant people through Moses or Isaiah, Paul applies to the Jews of his day. In verse 9 and 10, he cites the sixty-ninth Psalm. There the disciples had found a prophetic description of Christ suffering on Golgotha. What the psalmist says there about his tormentors Paul also applies to the Jews who tormented and killed their Messiah, Jesus Christ.

13–24, The Gentiles and Israel

Now Paul goes further. He has shown how only a remnant of Israel has been faithful, while the great majority has fallen. Now he shows what this apostasy has meant for the Gentiles and how it will finally go for the unfaithful people.

Thus Paul turns to the Gentiles. He also belongs to them. He is "apostle to the Gentiles," and he is proud of this. He is proud to be able to both serve the Gentiles and in this way possibly be able to "incite his kinsmen to jealousy" so that they understand what they are missing. Paul is firmly convinced that God has a good purpose for what has happened. Because Israel declined to receive the gospel,

---

[1] The ESV translates the term in question as "their full inclusion" with a footnote saying, "their fullness." The footnote would correspond better to Giertz's own translation.

it has gone out to the Gentiles, faster and with greater success than anyone could have imagined. Here Paul can speak from his own experience. Time after time, he had to say to the Jews, Since you thrust the message of God from you, so I go to the Gentiles (Acts 13:46, 18:6, 28:28). So this, that the Jews said no to Christ and crucified him, meant redemption for the world. Now if their rejection had such good consequences, what then shall not happen when they turn back and are established! This means that the "the dead may live!" By this, Paul means the resurrection and the new world will come. When Israel turns again, then God's plan with this world is fulfilled. And Paul is convinced that Israel shall turn back. Despite their apostasy, they are still God's chosen people. Paul takes the picture of "the dough of the first fruits," the bread that was baked with the year's first ears of grain and offered for thanks and as a sign that the whole year's harvest and every bread that is baked of it is consecrated to God. Paul takes another picture with the same contents: on a holy root grows a holy tree. The dough of the first fruits and the root correspond to the fathers of Israel. They were men of God, consecrated to God. They and their descendants have received God's promise. Therefore the seed that has fallen is also still *holy* in the word's original meaning: "consecrated and set apart to God to serve the purposes of God."

Paul warns the Gentile Christians from exulting over the Jews. It is certainly true that the church is now God's Israel. But a Christian is God's child and belongs to God's people because they are in grafted like a branch of a wild tree on a noble trunk, Israel's tree. When Paul uses this picture, he is, as so often, wholly ruled by the reality he wants to describe. He doesn't care that the image limps. In reality, it is a branch of a noble tree that is grafted onto the stem of a less noble kind. But on the contrary, here it is: it is the root and stem and sap that give worth to the foreign branch. Therefore the grafted branches should be careful about exalting over the branches that are broken off.

One can't escape thinking of how much in history would have looked differently if the "Christian" people had taken this seriously in their relationship to the Jews. Antisemitism, the persecutions and pogroms, would never have been. He who understands the gospel knows that the Jews still live under God's election. They may be His problem children, but they are no less loved for it.

Thus Paul reminds us that it was for the sake of its unbelief that some branches were cut off. And they who were remaining, original or engrafted, may remain for the sake of their faith, except they now cling to faith. And the branches broken off can be grafted back in again, if only they do not persist in their unbelief. Here we see that Paul's thoughts on election are not so conceived that salvation should happen automatically and that people themselves have no responsibility. One can push the gospel aside. One can persist in unbelief but also in the kindness of God. Paul does not say "persist in faith." This could lead us to look upon faith as something we perform, some sort of meritorious characteristic we ourselves do. No, this is about persisting in the kindness of God. Here comes an undeserved offer. This one can grab hold of, and one shall hold fast to it. We can never earn salvation, but we can very well lose it.

25–32, All of Israel Shall Be Saved

So Paul comes to that which this whole time he has seen as the background and the final goal of God's dealings with Israel. There is a mystery, a hidden council of God that has been revealed to him. As an apostle, he has been able to look into God's plans in order to be able to preach the gospel in all of His kingdom. And now he wants to speak about this mystery of God, so that the Gentile Christians should not become conceited in their knowledge (wise in their own eyes) and not imagine that they have any reason to look down upon the Jews. The hardening that has affected Israel is really something transient. It shall last only so long as the time of the world's missions lasts. There will come a day when the "whole harvest of the Gentiles has come in." This does not mean all people will have become Christians, but it means that the gospel will have reached out over the whole world and all who will receive it will have received it. God has no more to win. Then comes the final act. And in the end times of this world, all of Israel will be saved, as it has been foreseen by the prophets.

So Paul summarizes the Christian view of the Jews. If one looks at the gospel, then they are, for now and until later, enemies of God. Paul adds, "for your sake" and points to what he just said: what the Jews rejected has come so much sooner to the Gentiles. But if we look at election, they, the Jews, are still loved by God. God does not repent of His gifts and His calling. His mercy is not finished. So just as it came partially to the Gentiles, so shall the Jews also partake in it. God has "included them all under disobedience"; He has let the hardening affect them for the sake of their unfaithfulness and thanklessness. He has given His good to the Gentiles and made them into His people. But He has not forgotten the people He once chose. He keeps them alive and leads them in such hidden paths to a goal that He has determined. Therefore no one can eradicate them, and against all likelihood, they continue to make their way through history, to the goal that God has determined.

33–36, Psalm of Praise to the Unfathomable

Now Paul has reached the conclusion of the letter's chief part, where he puts forth the gospel. Like a pious Jew, he finishes with a "doxology," a praising of God. What he thanks God for is just that which the superficial common religiosity normally experiences as the major problem—what gives reason for so many bitter questions and accusations against God. God is inconceivable. We cannot understand how God operates. With Him, there is an infinite depth of wisdom and knowledge that we can never plumb. But he who encounters the living God knows that God is always right. He does not allow himself to lord over God. He gives no demands. Instead he is thankful that all rests in God's hand. He gives thanks that God knows and can do and does that which we can never fully comprehend, but that we know flows forth from the wellsprings of His kindness.

And so Paul gives one of the shortest and most content-rich descriptions that has ever been given of the Creator's work with us. With Him are all things. Without Him, there is only empty nothingness, that which is not even an empty space. From this nothingness, we have been called forth. Through Him, all things remain today only because in every new second He holds it together with His power; He who allows our pulse to beat and our consciousness to function. In the moment that He withdraws His hand, we are no more. And we now live to Him, perpetually on the path to the great encounter where it shall be revealed what we did with the life He gave us—if we who lived by Him, through Him, and to Him have also lived with Him and for Him.

Romans 12

1-2, Our Spiritual Temple Service

Now Paul begins the second chief part, that which contains admonitions. It is no accident that he lets the admonitions come last, after he has first spoken about what God has given us in Christ. Paul will not have any ambiguity. No one should believe that one can be Christian by following a series of good traditional rules. First comes what Christ has done for us, then comes what we should do for Him. And this that we do is never a condition, never a performance through which we earn the right to be God's children. Instead it is a consequence of what God does with us.

This becomes clear in what Paul says as an introduction to all his other admonitions. We shall complete our "spiritual temple service." Paul places it in contrast to the outward temple service that was active in the Old Testament. There one could sacrifice a sin offering. These were gifts that one brought forth to atone for his sin. But since Christ has offered Himself once and for all for the atonement of the whole world's sin, all such sacrifices are abolished. The only offering that remains is the thank offering. And this remains in that we offer ourselves to God in thankfulness for all that He has done for us. The sacrifice is not "spiritual" in the sense that it should be something that is only inward and invisible. It is our body that we are to put forth: our daily life, our work, the whole of our visible existence. It is a matter of a living sacrifice: the people themselves with all their power, with heart and soul. The offering is holy because Christ has sanctified it by His death. It would never have been "such as God would have it" if Christ had not atoned for all. Paul urges us "with the mercy of God" to bring forth this offering. We shall do it, not because we have a gift to come with that is worthy of God, but because God in His mercy allows us to be His children and come before His face.

When in this way a man surrenders himself to God over and over again, something happens with him. Instead of conforming to this world (as normally happens, if one is not formed by God), one is transfigured. Not instantaneously and not for all time, but one enters into the course of events that Paul described before (in Rom 8): the old man is disciplined and killed and the new life from Christ becomes a reality. One receives a new manner of thinking. One can judge everything in the light of God. One sees what His will is.

This is also the point of departure for all the admonitions that Paul gives now. He who lives in the communion of faith with Christ is reshaped by Christ. This is the only way to live a Christian life. One cannot set up a completely comprehensive instruction for Christian conduct with commands and prohibitions. But all can come into one such communion of life with Christ so that they begin to function in a Christian manner. And how one then lives can be described. One can give examples, reminders, and admonitions. This is what Paul does now.

3–8, Gifts of Grace

There is no standard model for a Christian. We are all different, and God has a purpose for these differences. There are different natural endowments, and there are different spiritual gifts. It is the latter that Paul now talks about. He begins with a warning against overvaluing some particular gift (or himself, if one has this gift). We are all members in Christ, and members must be different in order that the whole shall function. But we are "members of each other," as Paul literally says, thus members that are for each other and shall serve one another.

We have also received different gifts of grace. With "gifts of grace" (*charismas*), Paul means the particular gifts that the Spirit parcels out to everyone in the congregation "in such a manner that they can be useful," as he says in a different context (1 Cor 12:7). And here Paul gives a long series of examples of such charismatic gifts (just like in 1 Cor 12, where he mentions some of the same as mentioned here and moreover several others). Paul also gives a collection of examples in the form of a list. In the Greek text here, there are no direct admonitions (as in most of the translations) but only a statement of fact: such and such works this and that gift. But in this there actually lies an admonition also, and so Paul eventually passes directly over to exhortations. (Though the first example in the matter does not come before verse 14.)

What examples of charismatic gifts are they that Paul now mentions?

First comes prophecy, gifts to speak according to the Spirit's inspiration. Paul makes a little cautionary caveat: so long as faith is sufficient. He had apparently heard speech that passes itself off as being inspired but was not. There is false prophecy that is only human speech.

The next gift is to have a ministry or service. Paul uses the word *diaconate*, and it is possible that he is only speaking of the service of a deacon because the word had already received that special meaning. But it is just as possible that the word has its original meaning of "service" in the common use. In any case, one in the early church was convinced that all the church's ministries and offices came from God, that holders were gifts from Christ (Eph 4!) and that their ministry belonged together with the charismas (1 Cor 12:28).

The next thing to follow is "to be a teacher." In the New Testament, this always means to be a teacher of God's word, and in our day, this most closely corresponds to the pastoral ministry. The next thing on the list is to be a "comforter" or an "exhorter." It is the same word in Greek, from the same root as *Paraklete*, the name for the Consoler, Comforter, the Holy Spirit. Perhaps here it is not a matter concerning any particular office in the congregation but of a gift that can be found among some Christians. They are able to comfort by the authority in their word. This authority comes from one having gone through great sorrows and learning to take them from God's hand. These people could speak a word of exhortation with both love and firmness to those who needed it.

Behind these gifts that have been mentioned, one can imagine certain assignments in the congregation. But this need not be anything but common examples of how the Spirit works in everyday lives. When someone gives gifts, it happens from generosity, "without ulterior motives" (or from "upright hearts" as one could also translate it), without thought of being seen, without pretention from the giver. When someone does a service of mercy, then he does it with joy and doesn't ask if one deserves this or if they will be rewarded for trying to help them. "The leader" is perhaps a presbyter or a congregational leader. His gift of grace shows itself in that he goes to his task with all his heart and does not do his entrusted task with his left hand. He knows that he receives this task from the Savior. He fulfills it with love for Him, and he is blessed by that which he does.

9–21, The Love That Comes from Faith

With faith comes love: God's own love that is poured into our hearts. Paul has already said this (5:5). Now he describes how this love works. He still does it in the form of a description, though the whole time there lies an admonition in the word. One can hardly give a good translation without using imperatives (the verb form of admonition).

First, Paul says that the love shall be genuine, unfeigned—or rather that it is that if it is really a matter of agape: God's love, that which we receive as a gift. One can try force love from himself, but then it is not genuine, not spontaneous and immediate.

Love does not mean permissiveness, Paul continues. Love stands in an uncompromising opposition to all evil and holds uncompromisingly to good. Simultaneously, it is a real kindness. We "love one another from the heart with brotherly love." Here Paul does not use the same word as at other times, *agape*, but instead the word that was common among the Greeks when one spoke about care and love. Thus it is a question of the love that can be found among the Gentiles. What Paul wants to say is that the natural love within a family or relatives or circle of friends is deepened by Christ and expands its limitations so that the whole congregation becomes one great big family. This love causes one to give honor to each other naturally and without being asked. And this honor does not mean to flatter, but to give preference to the other person, to find it perfectly natural to defer to them when it comes to rank, duty, appointment, and reputation.

Love is not just a feeling of sympathy. Love is always being willing to step in and be available when something demands zeal and could mean difficulty, discomfort, and risks. It causes men to "burn in the spirit," to burn with a fire that warms those who need love but also can burn those who stand opposed to God. This love serves the lord—that is, Christ. It is according His being, a genuine love and a thankfulness, that He has served us. This makes us glad, always glad, because every day is filled by the great hope of Christ's return and His victory. He makes us patient in tribulation. What can separate us from Christ's love? This causes us to pray without ceasing. And all this shows itself in the midst of the congregation's unromantic everyday needs. Where there is love, one is active with relief services. Literally written, "Take part in the needs of the saints," where "the saints" are the Christians. Perhaps Paul is thinking of "the saints in Jerusalem" here, the poor original congregation that he diligently gathered money for. This means that Paul has included money and economic need as something that naturally belongs among the great spiritual realities: the hope, perseverance, prayer. It is no true faith that stands to the side with great words of the spiritual wealth. Faith is active in love and will immediately step into the realities of life with money and fund-raising, or willingness to receive guests in one's house. This manifestation of love had a great meaning in the early church where individual Christians, proclaimers, and others came visiting and needed to be taken care of—somewhat like travelers in ancient times—so they were put up and cared for in parsonages.

Paul continues with another harsh reality that could become real at any time: persecution. He points very openly to the words of Jesus in the Sermon on the Mount (Matt 5:44) but as usual does not cite it directly. This instruction, which the apostle "received" from the Lord and "submitted" to the congregations, was assumed to be known. Paul refers to it again and again. He develops and exemplifies, but does not repeat what all should know.

Then there follows a series of new examples of the life of love. It means that one can cry with those who cry. Tears also have their place in a Christian's life, just as much as joy. It means that one is not haughty and does not weigh with the scales of unbelief but "associates with the lowly"—or those who are "small," as the word can also mean. The admonitions to not give back what you receive and not to take revenge show how realistically Paul anticipates that this is a tempting thought even for the Christian. He runs the risk "of being overcome by evil," but he is called to overcome evil with good.

Romans 13

1–7, "The Christian and the State"

Does love have anything to do with the state now? For Paul and his contemporaries, the state was the Roman state. It had its virtues. It had obtained peace for the people and put an end to piracy and armed banditry, which were the scourge of the land in many places. It introduced Roman law and at least kept rudimentary order in check with power. But it was of the Gentiles. In questions of immorality, it was mostly permissible, and the rulers often led with poor example. It could also be quite harsh when it came to demanding taxes and tariffs.

The Christians knew that they had a better Lord than Caesar and that they were citizens in the kingdom of heaven. It was so close at hand that a Christian could feel that they were free from their duties to the Gentile state, as far as a person could presently avoid them. It is this tendency that Paul now turns his attention too. He reminds them that the state and legal system is a means by which God guides the world. God holds His creation with power also by allowing communities to occur where people are forced to take each other into account. Without society, anarchy would rule. Therefore God allows men to institute laws and establish governing bodies. This happens according to God's will. They who have received authority received a commission from God: they shall keep law and order with power. They shall promote what is good and set limits for violence and abuse. This task has nothing to do with salvation. It is not dependent on faith. It is enough that one makes use of the good instincts that God inscribed in human nature when He wrote that which the law demands in our hearts (as Paul said before in Romans 2:15).

The word that Paul used for the state used to be translated as "authorities." Essentially, it means "the powers" and thus the governing authorities—those who guide the land, from Caesar and his puppet princes (such as the tetrarch in Palestine) to their most subordinate officers. Paul says verbatim, "The powers who are in authority." The modern expression that best covers the meaning is perhaps "the lawful authorities." It is also a question of subordinate authorities who we have to deal with in our everyday dealings. Paul now speaks of taxes and tariffs.

The authorities also have their commission from God. They shall see to it that law and order prevail so that men can live in peace. Naturally, Paul doesn't mean that every functional state power actually carries out God's will in all that it does. They who have the authority can also betray their commission and be oppressors. On a personal level, they can be of poor character. But the actual legal system is from God, and one may not dispense with it. If they begin to shirk their responsibilities to the common good, they set themselves up against God's order. And this has consequences—consequences that the state has the right to execute. In essence, the state bears the sword. It will say, "Public policy must be argued coercively and even with weapons if needed."

Here Paul speaks about the Roman state as it then functioned. He does not take up the problem that we encounter in other areas of the New Testament: How does one act if the state becomes an instrument for evil and wants to directly uproot faith in Christ? The Christians in Jerusalem had already encountered this problem, and the answer was given: "One must obey God rather than man" (Acts 5:29). Soon the Roman state would come with demands that no Christian could fulfill. The Christians declined to obey and received martyrdom. The Book of Revelation teaches us that there comes a time when the legal system itself is in the hands of Satan, and then it only remains to confess your faith and take the persecution.

Neither is the rule that Paul puts forth here without limitations. It belongs to a greater context that characterizes the life in faith in Christ. A Christian subordinates himself. This means that he places himself under God's order. God has, both in creation and in Christ's new kingdom, firmly set certain good arrangements that the Christian willingly puts himself into. This also includes loyalty to the society in which a man lives, which does not mean a ban on any push for reform. If one lives in a democracy one is coresponsible for society's manner of being a servant of God. A man takes this responsibility seriously. If one lives without participation, perhaps under an atheistic regime, one may do as the Christians in the eastern states do: be loyal so far as it concerns the economy, property, and other external relationships but decline to participate in that which means that one denies Christ.

8–10, Love Is the Fulfillment of the Law

Paul turns back to love. When it comes to our earthly duties, then we shall fulfill them to the *T* so that we are not indebted to anyone. But when it comes to love, then we are never finished. There is always something more that we ought to do. He who is driven by love fulfills all the other commandments. Paul does not mean a feeling of love, a common benevolence, would be able to replace the other commandments. He means that we, if we are defined by the love of Christ, will carry out all this that the commandments want to safeguard. Because the Ten Commandments are formulated as prohibitions, Paul says that love fulfills them because it doesn't do anything against one's neighbor. Naturally, he means that it does something good instead.

11–14, The Day Is Near

Paul is always thinking of Christ when he admonishes. To live as a Christian is to live with Christ, before His face, consciously aware that the Risen One is near us and that He can reveal Himself in His glory at any moment. The hour is perpetually approaching. Initially, Paul was convinced that he and his contemporaries would see this day. Later he began to understand that it could delay. But the delay does not reduce vigilance. On the contrary, every day that passes means that we have come closer to the great day. Vigilance only increases. And what vigilance means is what Paul describes here: It is to encounter the light. It is to leave behind all that belongs to darkness. For most Gentile Christians, the past was literally a dark night of debauchery. One had lived for food, wine, and sex. It is typical for Paul that when he warns of all this, he immediately adds, "strife and envy." It is not only the coarse obscenities that are sinful. Daily pettiness and egoism are as equally serious in God's eyes.

The expression "pamper the body" has been chosen as the translation for some words that essentially mean "concern for the flesh." *The flesh* can mean both "the body" and "the old man." Perhaps here is meant "the body," but there is in the actual word choice a reminder of the "law of sin that lives in my members" that Paul spoke of before (Rom 7:23). Concern for the body is in and of itself something good. But it does not remain compliant or excessive in the manner that the old man wants. Then the control a Christian should have over both his body and his old man is jeopardized.

Romans 14

1–12, Weak Brothers and Strong

Now Paul takes up a special question that was burning in many congregations. This is also handled at length in First Corinthians (chapters 8 and 10). It dealt with what a Christian could eat and drink in good conscience, if he was able to work on the Sabbath, and so on. It was the same sort of question that we encounter today: Can a Christian drink wine, smoke, dance . . . ?

There were those who held that a restrictive and restrained line was the safest. In the early church, they were called "the weak." "The strong" were those who had sufficient faith to use their freedom without abusing it. Apparently, Paul felt closer in relation to "the strong." But he does not consider them right unconditionally. He doesn't make their line the acknowledged true one that every Christian should follow.

Apparently, "the strong" were the majority. There was even question of whether one could "receive" one who was weaker in faith. To "receive" meant to take him into their communion and welcome him to the Lord's Table. Here Paul gives a direct order: he shall be received as a Christian brother. And one shall not receive him in order to discuss this with him and show him that he is wrong. One shall let him follow his own path. One may not look down on him and think that he is narrow-minded and scrupulous. And "the weak" may not judge those who eat, which they apparently had a tendency to do. Paul obviously assumes that this concerns convinced Christians who all believe in Christ. He also assumes in all seriousness that "the weak" are not making their abstinence a law for all or a requirement for salvation. How inexorably Paul responded when someone tried to make the law a condition of salvation we can see in Galatians. He who does this has backslidden; he has fallen from Christ, Paul says. But if for his own reasons, on the ground of conviction of conscience, one refrains from such that others with good conscience use, then his conviction should be respected. The decisive thing is whether the man does this "for the Lord," even for the sake of Christ to preserve an uncloudy and sincerely honest relationship with Him. This means to both live and die for Him. Nothing may come between them. It may seem surprising that Paul mentions "dying for the Lord" here. Perhaps this is because immediately before this, there was the utmost distress and death in Ephesus, and in many other places, they were being brought together for persecution. The thought of death puts everything in proper perspective. The judgment seat of God does not delay long. And then it is for us ourselves, whom we shall give account, and not for others.

13–23, Concern for Others and Certainty for Themselves

With the great Day of Judgment before our eyes, we should quit judging one another. There is another judgment that is more important. This is our relationship to others. No one should do anything that causes his brother to fall. In First Corinthians, we can see how easily this was done. There were some things, such as meat that was offered to an idol and then sold, that for some was so insolubly connected to faith in idols that it could not be touched without experiencing it as an apostasy. Now if they saw a "strong" Christian, who with the best of intentions wanted to end their "prejudices" and determined despite everything to eat of such a thing, then the consequence could be total apostasy. As a contemporary parallel, one can imagine an open-minded person coaxing a (moral) absolutist to concede his position and how this will have dire consequences for his future. Such a thing cannot happen, Paul says. Certainly there is nothing that is unclean in and of itself. But if someone believes it is unclean and thus eats with poor conscience, then it injures him. One may not inflict injury on his fellow man in this manner. Paul is concerned about tangible worries and difficulties that really cause grief and can really pull a man into perdition. If one does so, one has abandoned love, the Lord Himself. It may not be that our good, the freedom we have in Christ, becomes exposed to critique and insult by our misuse. God's kingdom consists in more important things than food and drink. This does not mean that we can say that because it ultimately depends on righteousness and peace and joy, then we can use our freedom when it comes to external things and let the others say what they will. Paul draws the contrary conclusion: because we have righteousness, peace, and joy, we can abstain from the external things without missing them, and we ought to do this rather than risk injury to a weaker fellow Christian.

Thus the conclusion is this: let us strive after peace and edification. In the New Testament, edification always means that the church is built up, that the congregation is united and strong, that the individuals are built in like a living stone, firmly bound to Christ and with each other. One may not jeopardize this work of God for the sake of food, nor to hold their line in questions of alcohol or conscription or the sanctity of Sunday. Everyone may hold their line, under two assumptions: that "the weak" (perhaps we would say: the stricter, or more radical) do not judge and do not make their line into a binding law, and on the other side that "the strong" understand that perhaps not all can live as they do and that they may not do anything that draws another onto a path that means a warped relationship with Christ. Finally, it is all decisive that the whole time one is completely certain that one does everything before the face of Christ, as a good and faithful disciple under the Master's watchful eye. And then Paul formulates this pointed statement: everything done without faith is sin. The context shows what he means: everything that is done in unbelief with an uncertain or poor conscience, every action during which one does not want to think of Christ, is sin.

Romans 15

1–13, Mutual Respect Creates Mutual Concord

Paul counts himself as one of the "strong," they who have no compunction in questions of food and drink and the Sabbath or other external things. But precisely "we who are strong" are responsible to have respect for those who have concerns. We may not live as it pleases ourselves. Christ has given us a binding example, which Paul also speaks about in Philippians (2:5ff.): He who was like God emptied Himself to become like us. He became one of the "weak," a man like us. He who was God, high above all injury, stepped down and let the revilers have power over Him. All this He did for our benefit and edification.

When Paul cites the words of the Psalms concerning reproaches, he is saying that such old words are actually real. They are written with us in mind. There is a message for us that deals with Christ and us ourselves. It is through such words that scriptures give us comfort and make us resolute so that we can hold fast to our hope. God is really the God of steadfast comfort, the source of all our courage and endurance. It is He who can teach us to think the same thoughts in the manner that Christ wants us to think. This is what we need to be able to have respect for each other and overcome the difficulties that are connected with our different understandings. Then Paul advises, "Welcome one another"—that is, welcome each other in communion as siblings, just as Christ did with us, so we can celebrate real divine service, where we "of one accord and with one mouth praise our Lord Jesus Christ, God and Father." (It is not impossible that Paul is citing a piece of early Christian liturgy.)

This concord shall now unite Jews and Gentiles. So as God is fulfilling his promise to the fathers, he wants to simultaneously show mercy to the Gentiles, to whom no promises had been given. Paul cites four passages from the Old Testament that all say that even the Gentiles are called to worship Israel's God. They too have their hope in Christ, He who is the shoot from the stump of Jesse (even from David's trunk—Jesse is the Greek for Isai, who was David's father).

So God is also the God of hope for both Jews and Gentiles. And now Paul's desire for the Romans is that through faith in Christ they should be filled by the overflowing hope through the joy and peace that only faith in Christ can give. *Peace* here means, as so often, precisely the concord in the congregation that is the good concord and cohesion that Paul has in mind the whole time.

14–21, The Right of the Apostle to Admonish

After all these admonishments, Paul makes it clear that he certainly doesn't believe that everything is wrong with the Christians in Rome. On the contrary, he is convinced that they can take care of themselves. If they think that he has been too authoritative, they may remember that he is an apostle and has his commission from Christ. He is a "minister of Christ Jesus." The word *minister* does not mean the same as with us, "a congregation's shepherd and teacher," but it describes a sacrificial priest of the type that ministered in the Temple in Jerusalem. The New Testament really speaks of two types of priests. The one is characterized by proclamation, the servant of the word and the congregation's leader. Those of this type are called "shepherds and teachers," "presbyters" (from which we received the word "priest"), or "*episcopos*" (from which we received the word "bishop"). The other type is a sacrificial priest, they who would offer sacrifices and prayers in the Temple. They are denoted by a completely different Greek word that our Bibles have long translated as "priest." This place is the only one where Paul uses such terms for himself. Through Christ's sacrificial death, the whole old temple service had become superfluous. Christ is our great high priest and nothing else is needed. The only sacrifices that now remain are the thank offerings that mean that we offer ourselves as sacrifices to God, as Paul said before (Rom 12:1). But as apostle to the Gentiles, Paul may not only offer himself but also the Gentiles, those whom he has won for Christ, as a thank offering on God's altar. This is his priestly service.

In this service, he has now also received confirmation that it is God who works through him. Paul cannot escape seeing that, during the course of his missionary work, things have happened that would not have been believed possible. But he knows that it is Christ who has done it. All this he does through word and deed or through signs and wonders. That Paul carried out deeds that the rest of the world regarded as miracles is beyond doubt. Even his opponents had to recognize it, and he could point to it as one of the certified and witnessed facts (2 Cor 12:12).

22–33, Paul Presents His Travel Plans

Now Paul comes to his travel plans. As a transition, he mentions that he has always tried to break new ground and do missionary work where no other apostle has set foot. But now he is finished in the eastern half of the empire and sets his sights on the West. It can seem incredible that Paul considers himself to be finished when he knows that the congregations only make a thin strand of pearls stretching along the roads that he has traveled. But he has seen the inherent growth potential there is in the seed of the gospel, from Jerusalem to Illyria. Illyria was the Greek half of the empire's westernmost province, the present Dalmatia. Acts certainly makes no mention of Paul ever having worked there, but it is possible that he had time to make a detour there from Greece during his second and third missionary trips.

Now Paul aims for Spain. And on the way there, he will finally realize his desire of many years to come to Rome. He hopes that the Christians there will do what they have in all other places: give him travel funds to make it to the next city. Paul could rely on his tentmaking for his maintenance, but for the journey, he needs the help of the congregations. Apparently, it was counted as a self-evident duty of every congregation to help a traveling apostle make his trips. It belonged to the contemporary missionary offerings.

However, Paul first travels to Jerusalem to hand over the great gift to the congregation's poor that was gathered in Greece. (The Province of Achaia corresponds approximately to the southern half of our modern day Greece and Macedonia in the north.) It is a trip that Paul knows has its risks. So he asks for prayers, first for himself, that he shall be safe from the attacks of Jews (through which he really was about to get killed, though at the last second he was saved). Further, he asks for prayers concerning his own gift so that it should be received and strengthen the unity between Greeks and Gentiles, which was a matter of the heart for Paul.

Then something follows that looks like a conclusion, it is thought that Paul finished his dictation here and meant to send the letter as soon as there was a traveler who could take it with him. During the waiting time, some other things he wanted to say came to mind. Yet another page was fastened to the already long scroll, and the writer continues his work. But all such explanations—there are many—are and remain unproven guesses.

Romans 16

1–2, The Recommendation for Deaconess Phoebe

So Paul, if we dare to set forth a guess, has found a letter carrier with whom he can send his letter. He came to know that the deaconess Phoebe from the great city of Cenchreae (a harbor town of the great city of Corinth) will travel to Rome. So he sends the letter with her and simultaneously gives her his recommendation.

Now there are researchers who doubt this chapter originally belonged to Romans. A couple of details point to Ephesus, and some researchers have assumed it contains a small, independent letter written to the congregation there. There are examples of such short letter of recommendation preserved in papyrus as well as plain letters that consist of almost nothing but greetings. It is, however, hard to explain how such a letter to Ephesus should come to be included with a letter sent to Rome. Essentially, there is only one possible explanation, the one that was put forward at the beginning of the last century by an expert in the field (Adolf Diessmann): basically it is that Romans was copied right out of Paul's own book of drafts. There are preserved pieces of antique letter books where the owner kept copies of his own correspondence. These books of letters did not consist of scrolls, but of folded sheets sown together. Now if this little letter of recommendation came immediately after Romans by the same writer and under the same caption (which were often written with many abbreviations) and edges were accidentally obliterated by the page being cut, then a copier could have taken it for granted that it was from the same letter. This assumption—it is no more!—figures that at least some of what we have of Paul's letters we know to have been taken directly from his own book of drafts. Otherwise one normally supposes that they are copied from the receiving congregations, which were then given wider circulation. In any case, one knows that they were gathered at a very early stage. They are already cited diligently in Christian writings immediately after the year 100.

However, there are other researchers who have firmly held that this chapter originally belongs to Romans. There are strong reasons to adopt this. In letters to his own congregations, Paul doesn't otherwise greet individuals. But when he writes to Rome, he has reason to do this. This is a city he has never been to. He has reason to remind them of all his acquaintances there. And that Paul should know so many people in Rome is not anything to cause wonder. People often traveled, and Christians looked each other up wherever they went.

However, this chapter gives us a lot of small concrete insights into the life of an early Christian congregation.

First, applying to the diaconate, the recommendation is for a deaconess with the name of Phoebe (*Foibe* in Greek). Paul calls her "deaconess." This can mean servant, but one has reason to believe that here it is in view of a special diaconal service. Some years later, we see (in the letter to Philippians) that deaconess was already an established institution.

Now Phoebe leaves her home congregation in Cenchreae, and Paul advises the congregation in Rome to receive her in a manner "that is worthy of us Christians," "in the Lord," even as a Christian servant, as one should help in all areas where she needs help. This also assumes that they will feed her (as this will help her in her work), help where they can, and most of all, receive her as a sister in the family of Christ and as a cherished and much-needed coworker in the service of the Lord. Paul emphasizes that in her old place she had been a support for many, even for him. This shows an appreciation for the work of women in the congregation that he expresses time after time.

3–16, Greetings

There now follows an unusually long list of greetings. Because there are more individual names than in any other chapter in Paul's letters, it can be helpful to have a few explanatory words here concerning the forms names took in the New Testament. In Paul's world, there were many names with different origins, just as with us. Among the Greeks, one used Greek inflection, Greek spellings, and Greek accents. In this chapter, alongside truly Greek names (like Andronikos, Apelles, and Narkissos), there are some typical Roman names (like Rufus, Julia, and Urbanus) as well as an occasional Jewish name like Herodion and Maria. There are also several typical slave names: for example, Persis, Flegon, and Ampliatus.

When these names are rendered in a Swedish translation, one encounters some difficulties. As in all Western lands, we have from ancient times normally used the Latin forms that can distinguish themselves quite a bit from the Greek. This is because it was the Latin Bible that was used in the Western Roman Empire and knowledge of Greek died out during the Middle Ages. Today, if one wants to use the Greek forms, those that these men themselves used, one encounters the difficulty of emphasis (which can be on any of the last three syllables), and it often sounds incredibly foreign in our ears. We do not like to say Hermés or Apellés. The Latin has other accents that we are more familiar with. It is appropriate enough to use the Latin forms with Swedish spellings as a rule, but in another case the Greek form of the name is well known to us (e.g., Narkissos[1]).

In questions of emphasis, then, the rule is that it shall always be laid on the first syllable in a two syllable word. If the word has more syllables, than it can be either the second or the third from the end. It can thus be hard to know how one should pronounce such words, and therefore there is then a list of names with exposed accents in the back of our old Bible translation. In this chapter, we have these examples of names where the emphasis is three syllables from the end in the name: of Áquilla, Epénetus, Júnias, Herdion, Asýnkritus, Pàtrobas, Filólogus, Júlia, Timóteus, Lúkius, Sosípater, and Tértius. All the rest have the emphasis on the next to last syllable.

---

[1] These same issues occur with English translations.

Paul attempts to make his greetings warm and personal by strewing them with small comments and characteristics. They give us a living and challenging image of an early Christian congregation.

First, Paul names a woman, Priscilla. He names her before her husband, Aquilla. Paul had met them both in Corinth almost six years before. They had the same occupation as him, and he worked together with them for his maintenance. Then they followed him to Ephesus, where they stayed and worked for the gospel while Paul continued to travel. They must have been knowledgeable and wise. When the learned Apollos came to Ephesus and preached concerning Jesus, they noticed a lacuna in his knowledge and then "they took him and instructed him thoroughly in the way of God." (In the story about this [Acts 18:26], the wife is also named before the man.)

We don't know at which occasion they "risked their necks" to save the life of Paul. It was probably in Ephesus, where Paul, as he says in the beginning of Second Corinthians, was close to getting killed, as happened so many times before. Paul does not neglect to point out in passing that it was two Jews who did the Gentiles the service of saving the life of their apostle. As so often, Paul also mentions "those who are gathered in their house." In the great city, the church functioned as small "house churches." The Christians who had enough space voluntarily donated their home as a meeting place. On particular days, already at this time "the first day of the week," thus Sunday, they gathered in such a manner that all the small groups came "to the same place" in order to hold a common service with communion.

Paul sends the next greeting to the man who was the first to be baptized in "Asia," which here means the province of Asia—also the countryside around Ephesus. Then he greets someone unknown to us, the little Maria "who worked so hard for their sake." This is already the third woman Paul has mentioned in this chapter, an example of the role that women played in the work of the congregation and of Paul's estimation of their contribution.

Then there follows a pair of men "who are well known to the Apostles." It can mean that they were esteemed among the leaders of the church. It can also mean that they themselves were called apostles. *Apostle* was really the Greek word that corresponded to a Hebrew word that meant "authorized envoy." One could, like Paul and the twelve, be an apostle of Jesus Christ. But one could also be an envoy for congregations, sent out as a missionary or to carry out some other commission. So those, for example, who carry the gathered gift to Jerusalem are called "apostles" (2 Cor 8:23). Paul calls both these men his "fellow prisoners." Perhaps this means that they were locked in prison with Paul on some occasion. Paul had been detained on several occasions that we know almost nothing about.

Then follows name after name. Many are mentioned as coworkers. As we saw in the twelfth chapter, all the practical cares of the congregation are counted as the Spirit's work. To be a helper or coworker in the apostle's work also included such things as lending one's home, providing bread and wine for the divine service, receiving traveling Christians, providing food for the poor or care for the collections, and much more. We hear of Apelles that he "stood the test as a Christian." Here we don't know in what way, perhaps during some persecution. The greeting "to those with Narkissos who are Christian" could mean that Narkissos, a master and employer, was not a Christian himself—or that he was one but only some in the family or among the household were.

Again Paul mentions women: Tryfena, Tryfose, Persis. They have worked hard for Christ. A second old woman has been like a mother to him. He mentions another couple. Talk of Paul as a woman hater is on poor ground. He has both seen and promoted as well as appreciated the contributions of women. That he was simultaneously opposed to them being "teachers" and shepherds for the congregation could only be because he was bound by God's law and Christ's command.

Paul finishes with the admonition that the congregation should exchange the holy kiss, the sign of the siblings between all believers. The letter would be read at the divine service, where the kiss of peace belonged.

17–20, A Handwritten Greeting from Paul

Now follow a few lines that are set apart from the preceding by sharpness in tone. This has caused some commentators a degree of difficulty, especially when one assumes that Paul worked in approximately the same way as a present author, with pen in hand and a draft or an outline in front of him. In fact, he dictated for a writer, possibly walking around in a room. We can assume that it happened with many interruptions as people came and went. Now it could happen—we see it clearly in Galatians (6:11ff.)—that Paul finally set himself down, grabbed the pen, and wrote a handwritten greeting. In Galatians, we see that it could be impulsively and drastically formulated. It is possible that here it also has to do with such a loaded concentration of that which perpetually panged Paul's heart: fear that his opponents, those who did not understand the gospel, would successfully destroy the young churches. He warns of them here. It can be a question of *Judaizers*—they who want to make the gospel into law. It can possibly be some other deviation, possibly some of those that Paul corrects in the letters to Corinth and Colossae. He does it with the same sharpness he uses in many other places: False teachers are not innocent deceivers. It is a mortal danger. If one cheats the gospel, then all is lost. It is Satan who wants to destroy. God is the God of peace, who wants concord through fidelity to the unadulterated gospel.

21–27, Added Greetings and Final Wish

Again Paul leaves the pen to his writer and sends a couple of greetings, possibly from people who just found themselves in the room. The first is Timothy, his most faithful coworker. Then follow three others, of whom Sosipater may be the same person who follows Paul to Jerusalem a little later. (Acts 20:4 mentions a "Sopater," a variant of the same name.)

Now the letter is almost finished, and Tertius, who served as writer, fits in a pause to send his own greeting. Then there come a few more people who ask to send greetings. First it is the host there, Gajus, who received the title by keeping his house open for all his fellow Christians. In First Corinthians, we hear that Paul personally baptized a Gajus in Corinth, and it is possible that the apostle now lives with the same man. Later there comes a greeting from one of the city's service men and finally a few Christians unknown to us.

Now at the end, there follows the solemn final greetings, with thoughts that are encountered again in Ephesians. The gospel is the message of Christ, the great mystery that is revealed in just this time and is now preached according to the scriptures and according to God's commission so that all people shall be carried to the obedience of faith. Thus the letter ends with a line that refers back to the starting point: the gospel is God's power of salvation, an offer from God that shall be received by faith.

About the Author

Bo Giertz (1905–1998) was a Swedish Lutheran apologist, theologian, bishop, and, above all else, pastor. While similar in many ways to lay theologians C. S. Lewis and G. K. Chesterton, Giertz spent his life in professional church work upon his conversion from atheism. He trained as a theologian under one of the greatest exegetes of the last century, Anton Fridrichsen, at the University of Uppsala. Much to the disappointment of Fridrichsen, Giertz did not pursue a PhD. In fact, after spending half a year in Palestine in 1930, Giertz cut his academic career short to pursue parish life. He would later use the diaries, notes, and memories of that six-month excursion to write *With My Own Eyes*. It was on that trip to Palestine that both Giertz and Fridrichsen gave up on interpreting the New Testament text through higher criticism. This shared experience would lead to a lasting friendship between Giertz and Fridrichsen. After changing his hermeneutics, Giertz came to love the Greek text deeply. Learning later in life that he was going blind, the bishop read his Greek New Testament aloud into cassette tapes so that when he could no longer read Greek, he could at least listen to it.

Giertz always wanted to remain true to the scriptures he loved, because in them, he heard the loving voice of his Lord, Jesus Christ. This desire to remain true to the scriptures never manifested itself in legalistic or fundamentalist notions. However, it would lead him sometimes to take unpopular positions that would cause him hardship among his colleagues. It was with great sadness that he watched the confession of his church deteriorate through the years. Before he died, Giertz remarked that the Church of Sweden, where he served as a bishop, would no longer be able to ordain him if he applied then to be a parish pastor. He saw that few understood scripture or the Christian faith anymore, even among faithful churchgoers. He understood the need for the law of God, but he also understood obedience to the law could not be compelled outside the work of the Holy Spirit in and through the forgiveness of sins won for us through Christ Jesus. So as a retired bishop, he set about a great exegetical task of writing a commentary on the entire New Testament. Giertz hoped his commentary would be beneficial for laymen: short and easy to read, scholarly in its research yet devotional in its content, and focused on Christ—the word of the cross that is the power of God.

About the Translator

Bror Erickson is currently a pastor in the Lutheran Church–Missouri Synod serving the parish of Zion Lutheran Church in Farmington, New Mexico, where he lives with his patient and beautiful wife, Laura.

As the son of a pastor and missionary, Erickson has traveled extensively and was introduced to many different cultures, customs, and perspectives early in life. By the age of eight, Erickson had lived in four countries on three continents and in three states. This led him to an appreciation of foreign languages, beginning with German (because it is the language of Luther) in high school.

After quitting high school early, he worked on a ranch in central Montana before joining the air force. During his time serving, Erickson also attended school to become an electrician for the civil engineers. He spent most of his time with the air force in northern Italy and received the NATO Medal for Operations in former Yugoslavia. While in Italy, Erickson both decided to become a pastor and fell in love with the works of Giertz after receiving a copy of *The Hammer of God* from his father.

Six years later, while at seminary, Erickson began to study Swedish upon learning that most of Giertz's oeuvre remained untranslated. He now spends an inordinate amount of time translating so that the works of Giertz do not remain out of reach for the English-speaking world.

www.ingramcontent.com/pod-product-compliance
Lightning Source LLC
Chambersburg PA
CBHW071747080526
44588CB00013B/2172